A Voice From Heaven
Lessons My Son Taught Me

By
Charles J. Wisdom

Copyright © 2006 by Charles J. Wisdom

A Voice From Heaven
by Charles J. Wisdom

Printed in the United States of America

ISBN 1-60034-702-9

All rights reserved solely by the author. The author guarantees all contents are original and do not infringe upon the legal rights of any other person or work. No part of this book may be reproduced in any form without the permission of the author. The views expressed in this book are not necessarily those of the publisher.

Unless otherwise indicated, Bible quotations are taken from the New International Version of the Bible. Copyright © 1995 by The Zondervan Corporation.

www.xulonpress.com

Endorsements

"I highly recommend his story to anyone who is struggling with his or her own sexuality. This is indeed a story of redemption."
Ed Young, Pastor
Second Baptist Church Houston

"The story of Charles dealing with his son ought to be a handbook in the hands of Christian counselors and pastors. Van Wisdom proved that great calamities can bring great glories."
T. W. Hunt
Author, Retired Seminary Professor

"When Van and I reconnected 10 years later at an Exodus conference, and both of our struggles with homosexuality were revealed, our friendship was refreshed and deepened. Van was a bright spot in my life and in the lives of many."
Michael Goeke, Executive Vice President
Exodus International

"A Voice From Heaven will be worth your time to read and consider."
E. D. Hodo, President
Houston Baptist University

TABLE OF CONTENTS

Dedication ix

Preface xi

PART I: A JOURNEY OF A THOUSAND MILES

Foreword xv
1. Early Years 17
2. Restoring The Years 31
3. The Road Back Home 45
4. Joy And Grief Together 59

PART II: LESSONS MY SON TAUGHT ME

5. "Life Is Not A Dress Rehearsal" 77
6. Lessons Van Taught Me 91
7. Vanisms 99
8. "Though He Is Dead, He Is Still Speaking…" 111
9. Sermons From The Heart 117
   "The Prodigal Son" 117
   "The Prodigal Father" 127
   "Men Restoring The Walls" 142

PART III: A VOICE FROM HEAVEN

Foreword 161
10. A Voice From Heaven 167
11. Time And Eternity 177
Foreword to Chapter 12 191
12. Questions And Answers 193
13. Soon, And Very Soon 207

References 225

DEDICATION

This book is dedicated to the many people who were touched by Van Wisdom's life.

PREFACE

During Van's illness and immediately following his death in February of 2002, there were hundreds of letters and e-mail messages sent to him or to our home. The ones found in this book represent only a small portion of these treasured testimonies.

It seems to us that Van was chosen of God to influence many people. He was highly gifted by the Holy Spirit to give love and encouragement, and he did it on a much broader scale than he, or we, ever thought possible.

Van would not want to take the credit or the glory for anything he did. He knew God had performed a miracle in his life and helping others was a natural overflow of gratitude on his part.

Van, I love and miss you!
Mom
(Lilly Faye Wisdom)
Christmas 2002

PART I

A JOURNEY OF A THOUSAND MILES

FOREWORD

When beginning any journey, it is helpful to know not only where you are going, but where you are coming from, as well. As Bilbo once remarked to Frodo, "It's a dangerous business . . . going out of your door. You step into the Road, and if you don't keep your feet, there is no knowing where you might be swept off to."[1]

Well, I shall try to be careful and not get "swept" away, as it were. I want to share with you about my son, Van, and how God did a mighty and amazing work in his life. In order to do that, I feel I must share some of our family's history to help the reader understand where Van "came from." You will note that some chapters end with letters written to us after his death. I included these as another way to show what an amazing life my son had.

Join me now, as we set off down that road to the past.

CHAPTER 1—EARLY YEARS

Lilly Faye and I met as freshmen attending East Texas Baptist College in Marshall. She was the first girl I dated there, and we married the summer before our junior year. Six months after we were married, I became pastor of the Clawson Baptist Church in Lufkin. We were very young; I was twenty-one years of age and inexperienced. Lilly Faye was only twenty years old. However, the people of the Clawson community and church welcomed us and we were honored to serve that church for six and a half years. During that time, with support from Lilly Faye and the Clawson Baptist Church, I graduated from college and seminary.

Commuting to Fort Worth, where Southwestern Seminary is located, was a challenge. I would leave Monday night, live in the men's dormitory during the week, and return home on Friday afternoon. The difficulty of this was made easier as Lilly Faye's family was only an hour's drive away. Lilly Faye and Carla Faye (our daughter, born in 1961) would stay with her family during the week and then come back to the parsonage when I returned home on Friday. Also helping were the loving families of our church. Many of these people saw Lilly Faye and me as kids who needed lots of assistance (which we did!). If Lilly Faye or Carla Faye became ill, there were at least a dozen older women who would move in to stay with them, cook and care for them, and just take over the house. They even drove them to the doctor for appointments. I hated being away from them and considered dropping out of seminary. Lilly Faye, her family, and the ladies of the church would not hear of it.

On October 6, 1965, Van Joseph Wisdom was born at the Memorial Hospital in Lufkin, Texas. We named him after our dads — Alonzo Joseph Wisdom and Van Buren McKinney. Dr. Anna Connell, the same doctor who had delivered Carla Faye, also brought Van into the world.

When he was three months old, we moved to Wichita, Kansas where I became pastor of the University Baptist Church. We began our ministry there on the first day of January 1966, and left Wichita on the last day in December 1967.

Besides college, this was the first time we had lived away from our parents. The cultural setting for ministry was quite different from what we had known in East Texas. With some exceptions, the people in the University Baptist Church of Wichita were from everywhere *except* the Midwest. Few were natives of Wichita and there was a high degree of transience in the church. People were constantly moving in and out for work or to study at Wichita State University, which was located just across the street from the church. We had never had that kind of rapid mobility environment in which to serve. In addition, it was the time of the Vietnam War and the spirit of the 60's was questioning all traditional or "establishment" institutions. In spite of the difficult time we had in adjusting to our new working and living environment, there were wonderful people in the church who loved us and followed our leadership. The church grew and we were able to build a badly needed worship center during those two years. Many of the people who served with us at the University Church are still good friends to this day.

MISSIONARIES TO MEXICO

One of our life-long goals was to serve as missionaries with the Foreign Mission Board of the Southern Baptist Convention. Little did we know that to the day, two years after beginning our ministry in Wichita, we would be appointed to serve in Mexico with the Mission Board. After spending four months in missionary orientation at Ridgecrest Conference Center in North Carolina, we left for the Spanish Language School in Guadalajara, Jalisco, Mexico. Our first year was spent in getting a grasp of the language and culture. We then began working with Mexican university students. In addition, we were administrators of two dormitory-type homes for students. I taught English at the University of Guadalajara in the School of Philosophy and Letters. I also served as interim pastor of the English-speaking Gethsemane Baptist Church in Guadalajara.

A couple of years after arriving in Guadalajara, Lilly Faye and I accepted the leadership of an English-speaking student/youth ministry called "Saints." Kay Arthur, founder of Precepts Ministry, had started this work. When she and husband Jack returned to Tennessee to develop their new ministry, she asked me to give leadership to the young people. We met twice a week with the students and would venture out into the country for weekend retreats three or four times a year.

In all this, my family was heavily involved. "Saints" met in our home weekly, and Lilly Faye, along with Carla and Van (later Rose, when she was born to us in 1970) would go to the retreats with us to help out in a variety of ways. We always had twenty-five to fifty kids, plus four to eight adults as teachers and helpers at these retreats. By and large, these were great times for our family and for our ministry.

However, something horrible happened during a couple of those retreats. Lilly Faye and I did not learn about these things until over twenty years later. One or more of the boys sexually molested Van when he was around six or seven years of age. Fearful, ashamed, and feeling maybe it was his fault, Van kept this secret to himself until after he graduated from college.

All through junior high and high school, Van struggled with an arrested sexual development. This is a common result of sexual molestation. Depending on whose statistics one turns to for data, sixty-five to ninety percent of all male homosexuals were sexually molested as children or adolescents. Most authorities on the subject of male homosexuality insist that there are other factors in leading a male to have same-sex attraction, but they are in agreement that this is one of the major contributors to sexual orientation confusion.

A Voice From Heaven

I'm happy to report that Van and our family had hundreds of good experiences while living in Guadalajara and, later, Mexico City. It is only right that some of these be mentioned. To this day, our family has wonderful memories of our time in Mexico.

Van was an excellent swimmer. When we came home on furlough, he was nine years old, and Lilly Faye and I enrolled him in a swim club near our home. His coach was impressed with his desire and innate capabilities. His swim coach encouraged us to keep him involved in the sport because he saw great potential in him.

When we returned to Mexico City after furlough, Van became a member of a competitive swim club and was immediately thrown in with kids who had been swimming competitively for years. In the beginning, it was very difficult for him. The coach would end each day's practice with a series of free-style races. At the end of the each race, the winner was permitted to leave the pool area and get dressed to go home. Then, all the other swimmers would race again with the same procedure. For the first two weeks, Van was the last kid to finish in each race. This was extremely difficult for him. Not only did he have the pain of always being last, but also he had to repeat the exhausting race with each one more difficult than the last. By the time they completed six or seven of these races, the coach would allow the rest of the kids to leave the pool and get dressed. Van was physically spent after each of these workouts. However, he persevered and developed such stamina that he was always out of the pool after the second or third race.

His coach mentioned to me that he was sorry Van was not a Mexican National; he felt our son had potential to reach Olympic status if he maintained his interest in the sport. What a thing to hear about your child! We were very proud of him. When we finally returned to Texas, Van continued to swim and eventually helped his high school team win the state championship two years in a row. He could have been part of a college team if he wanted, but his interest in the sport began to wane.

During those years in Mexico, like the majority of boys his age, Van was curious about many things. Family members and friends have laughed on many occasions about how the boy could

A Voice From Heaven

talk without ending, with much of the discussion being questions about various aspects of life. In addition, he was extremely bright and surprised people from time to time with his answers. On one occasion, when he was four years old, missionary friends visiting our home were commenting on his cute baby sister. Without looking up from the activity in which he was engaged on the floor, he loudly replied, "Yeah, she is cute. But she can really mess up her diaper!"

One Sunday after church, three missionary families went to a restaurant to have lunch. As is common in Guadalajara's year-round excellent weather, this particular café had tables outside. We decided to eat on the large patio that would give the kids a chance to play after they had finished eating, allowing the parents a chance to visit.

On the front sidewalk of the café there was a caged monkey. Naturally, that was a big attraction for the missionary kids who laughed at his antics. Suddenly, the kids began to scream. "The monkey has got Van!" they yelled. I jumped up with the other dads to run over and see what was going on. Evidently, Van had stood too close to the cage and the monkey had reached through the bars and wrapped his tail around Van's leg. By the time I got to the cage, Van was terrified and some of the children began to cry. I grabbed my son around the waist and began to pull on him, but the monkey held on tightly. Then, he simply let go and Van was free! All of this took place within moments, and immediately the tears and frightened faces turned to laughter and smiles. Even Van began to smile and laugh out loud at what had happened.

Another good memory we have of our son in Mexico is that he loved to sing. He and Carla went to the Lincoln School in Guadalajara and the American School in Mexico City. There were many student presentations when parents and friends were invited to come and see their children's performances. Van often had singing parts in these presentations. Actually, he gained a little "fame" among the families of the Lincoln School, particularly for his rendition of the hymn "Holy, Holy, Holy." As a first grader, when he hit the high notes of the song, the blood vessels in his throat would swell to a size three times larger than normal and the contortions on his face were certain to hold everyone's attention.

Van and Carla sang together on several occasions. She learned to play a few songs on a baritone ukulele and they would entertain friends of groups when we visited churches while on furlough. They also learned to do the famous Mexican Hat Dance and, wearing national costumes, they were a crowd pleaser at the churches we visited.

THE WINDY CITY

During furlough, we moved to Chicago so I could finish my doctoral studies at the Chicago Theological Seminary. Van was in second grade that year, and he indicated his desire to have Believer's baptism. I talked with him at length about his interest in receiving Christ into his heart and life and, when he was eight years old, I baptized him. It was a glad time for Van; in later years he would reference the time he gave his heart to Jesus Christ as Savior and Lord.

During our time in Chicago, Van played on a Little League baseball team and also took karate lessons. He played left field, and while his performances were not stellar, he did okay. However, I clearly remember one occasion when we were playing an important game. A strong hitter came to bat and our coach motioned for Van to back up, deeper into the outfield. This kid still managed to blast a shot over Van's head. I heard the coach moan as it seemed clear this was going to be an in-the-park homerun. To our delight, Van caught up with the rolling ball, scooped it up, and fired it to the shortstop. Meanwhile, the batter was rounding third base and heading home. The shortstop threw the ball to our catcher and the runner was shocked to see the catcher standing at the plate, ready for him. The homerun turned into an out. I was so proud of Van and he was one of the heroes of the game.

The interest in karate did not last long, but it served Van well. As is often the case, the school bully wanted to let the new kid know who was boss and immediately began to badger Van. After the second or third time of being pushed around, Van hit him in the nose with one of his best karate chops and, from that time on, he never had any more problems with that kid.

MEXICO CITY

In 1974, after finishing my studies, we moved to Mexico City and I began teaching in the seminary. I also became interim pastor of the Capital City Baptist Church. There, we met wonderful people from the United States, Canada, England, and others who wanted to worship in English. Some of these people are our friends to this day, and we have enjoyed visiting their homes, as well as having them with us in our home. Moreover, the church had several missionaries who were associated with the Wycliff organization, whose Hispanic America headquarters were located near Mexico City. This large compound was a small town within itself and we loved going there each Saturday to spend the day with our new friends. Our kids were able to run freely and play with the many children and young people that lived in the compound.

SAN ANTONIO, TEXAS

In 1976, after eight years associated with the Foreign Mission Board of the Southern Baptist Convention, we moved back to Texas permanently. Lilly Faye and I had determined the Lord was leading us back into the ministry of pastoring a church. We settled in San Antonio where we served the Shearer Hills Baptist Church. It was the beginning of over nine years of very happy ministry in a city we came to love dearly.

A NORMAL KID?

Van seemed to live two lives as an adolescent. It was not something we noted with clarity; we chalked it up to usual teenage moodiness. Moreover, he was the middle child and we were told that this might make him feel left out in some ways. His older sister was smarter, had more opportunities, etc. His younger sister was the "baby" of the home and enjoyed those unique privileges.

On the other hand, our son had the most winsome personality and could entertain family and friends at the drop of a hat. As he entered the final two years of high school, he began to assert himself more and dated frequently. He played on the school tennis team in addition to being on the swim team. By the time he had finished high school, Van was very well liked and had many friends, both male and female.

Of course, there was the usual growing up difficulties to face with Van. On one occasion, when I was attending a church function in another state, he went out with a group of friends on a Friday night and did not return home until 3:00 A.M. His mother was frantic as his curfew was 12:30 A.M. on those nights. Since I was not there, she called a neighbor who was also a friend and member of our church. She was afraid he had been involved in a car accident, or something worse. This good neighbor said he would drive around town and maybe find someone who had seen Van or knew if something had happened that night. After doing so, he returned to tell Lilly Faye that he had learned nothing. Not too long after that, Van walked through the door. He and his buddies had gone to a late movie, then to an all-night diner to eat, and he simply let the time get away from him. When I got home, we decided that he would be grounded for two weeks. He didn't like it, but had no choice.

When he was a junior in high school, Van went to a football game with two friends. Lilly Faye and I had season tickets to the games, but had stayed home. About an hour-and-a-half later, we heard a knock on the front door. When I opened it, there was Van and one of his friends. Van was bleeding at the mouth. His friend explained that there had been some "horse play" at the game and things had gotten out of control. One of the guys hit Van in the mouth, loosening one of his teeth. We immediately called Van's dentist, who was also a friend. He met us at his office and repaired the tooth.

There were two things that really interested Van, apart from his school activities. One was learning to drive a car. I gladly took on that task and saw it as a way for us to spend time together doing something he wanted to do so badly. It was a very good experience for both of us. I had just bought a small sports car and let him drive it to school every once in a while, making it even more fun for him.

House construction is the other thing in which Van was very interested. He enjoyed walking through houses that were being built, and there were several times he and I would walk around our growing community, looking for houses under construction. It made me think he might one day become an architect. While that did not happen, he remained interested in the building business for most of his life.

A major influence in our son's life was a young lawyer in our church who taught Van's Sunday School class. This man was a great model for the high school boys in his class and he invested a lot of time in their lives. When he heard years later of Van's death, he called to offer condolences and freely wept as he lamented the death of one so young and so highly talented. Lilly Faye and I have often thanked God for the people who influenced our son during those formative days of his life. I am convinced this is one of the tools God used to eventually free Van from his inner turmoil. Then, to add greater joy to victory, the Lord used him in a marvelous way with people who struggled with serious inner pain.

BAYLOR UNIVERSITY

When he left for Baylor University, he exploded with vitality and personality. He was "Mr. Everything" as he plunged into academic and social activities. An article in Baylor University's Student paper, The Lariat, dated April 1987 tells about how he won a trip to the Cayman Islands, two Suzuki mopeds and two days at a retreat spa. The mopeds were for him and for his younger sister, Rose, who would be entering Baylor the following year. The trip to the retreat spa he intended to give to his older sister, Carla, and her husband, Scott Robinson. This he was able to accomplish by leasing out thirty-five apartments at an apartment complex near the Baylor campus. The apartment manager told The Lariat, "It would take a professional to lease out as many apartments as he did. It's his charisma—he's loaded with it."

Van was very popular with fellow students, dated frequently, and became very interested in a young lady who had come to Baylor from out of state. He later told me that there was a time when he knew without a doubt that he loved this girl and dreamed of marrying her. He even went to see her after he began to get his life straightened out, only to be broken-hearted to learn that she was engaged to marry a young seminary student. I will always remember when he returned home from that trip. He was depressed for a couple of weeks; it was as though he had missed his great chance.

His junior year, Van was elected a yell-leader at Baylor. It was a thrill for him; he had always enjoyed gymnastics and was very strong and agile. The following summer, he worked for the National Cheerleaders Association of America and traveled from campus to campus around the country, teaching and judging cheerleader camps.

It was during that time he met two young men to whom he was strongly attracted. He later told me that those two young men introduced him to other fellows who were determined to convince him that he was, in fact, born with the "homosexual gene," and he could no more deny that reality than he could deny his brown eyes. The combination of sexual uncertainty, attraction to these young men who were witty and seemed to be having the time of their lives, plus his propensity to always look for fun led him step by step into the homosexual lifestyle. That was his junior year at Baylor and for the following three years he increasingly pulled away from his family as he entered more deeply into a dark world that seemed to him to be his destiny. During this time, he kept this information from his family and other friends. As he said in a testimony to the First Baptist Church of Katy, Texas, as well as many of the other speaking opportunities he was given the last years of his life, "I was so ashamed, filled with guilt, and deeply confused. I didn't know what to do, but I knew what I *could not do: I could not hurt my family and many friends and tell of my deep, dark struggles. I did as my homosexual friends did; I covered my pain with more and more laughter and fun.*"

SPAIN

After graduating from college, Van worked for a year to save money so he could move to Barcelona, Spain. His goal was to live in

Europe where he could do whatever he wanted without restraints and without the possibility of shaming his family or hurting me professionally. One of his greatest fears was that I could lose my ministry if word got out that he was involved in a same-sex attraction lifestyle. (I confess to that same fear when I first heard the truth about all this. My first reaction was to resign from the ministry, move to another city, and begin a new professional life. Now I understand this old, old tactic of our adversary, Satan: to confuse and ruin by intimidation and fear. More on that later.)

In Barcelona, there was a period of about two years that Van ran with a "bohemian" crowd. These were young men and women like himself from Germany, Sweden, France, England, and Spain. They lived more or less in communes, taking care of one another. Van worked at one job after the other, teaching English or aerobics and gymnastics.

One of the interesting and encouraging aspects of his time in Spain was his deep desire to periodically slip away to church. Two churches in particular meant much to him: a certain Catholic church and a Baptist church of around 400 active members. When Lilly Faye and I visited him toward the end of his stay there, he took us to both places. I asked about his interest in the Catholic Church and he said the beauty and serenity of the place was a magnet that drew him there once or twice a week. The church was located in a part of Barcelona where many of the past artists of the city, some of them famous painters or architects like Picasso and Gaudi, would gather to drink coffee and eat *tapas*.

He loved to go there to sit and meditate all alone, he said. Looking back and having the experience of entering into heart-to-heart discussions with him after he left the homosexual lifestyle, I now know that Van was in deep turmoil. There was a strong pull on his heart—one toward the world, and the other to what he had known as a young boy at home, a life he loved and missed dearly. Meditating in that Catholic church, Van was able to find serenity.

When he became lonesome for his family, or deeply perplexed about his desperate state, he would go to the Baptist church. The pastor of the church, when we met him, pleased us greatly when he told us about how much he appreciated Van and that the people in the church who knew him liked him a lot. That helped us know he had not just gone there that one time to impress us. It also made me wonder if maybe Van had sought out the pastor for counseling. Van believed that sometime toward the end of his second visit to Barcelona he was infected with the HIV virus, but it would be over a year after he returned to Houston before he tested positive.

WHY? WHY? WHY?

I have wondered countless times about why Van had an attraction to homosexuality. He and I had sought counseling in Houston with Rev. Michael Newman, founder and counselor with "The Christian Coalition For Reconciliation." Michael was deeply involved in the homosexual lifestyle for many years. Then, through the power of Christ, Christian teachings, and the help of loving and wise people, he was able to break away from this way of living. For the past twenty years he has been helping people who, either they or their family members, struggle with homosexuality. If they want assistance in finding a way out, Michael and those who work with him provide counseling, referral to support groups and, above all, spiritual support. When we started seeing Michael, I wanted help for Van, but I was also desperate to get help for myself. I felt so guilty; it was hard for me to pass a day without asking myself how and where I had failed as a father. I knew that one of the contributing factors to a boy being attracted to homosexuality was a passive or absent father. According to this part of the explanation as to why homosexuality occurs, at strategic times in his psychosexual development, a boy does not fully "bond" with his dad. There may be genuine love that both father and son have for one another, but like the two proverbial "ships passing in the night," the two male personalities simply don't "click" in ways that helps the boy to grow in his sense of male identity. If there is no male figure with whom he can identify, or he has a mother, sisters, or other significant females who are strong and domineering in his life, this may lead him to subconsciously identify with females and even begin to talk and/or express himself in effeminate ways. (This latter aspect of homosexuality never became a part of Van's *persona*.)

There came a time when Van and I, both in counseling and in heart-to-heart discussions, were able to talk freely about these concerns. Always one to accept his responsibility for whatever choices he had made in life, Van continually reassured me that my lack of "being there for him" was not as big a factor as I allowed it to be. He would remind me of how I never missed his swim meets, or when I helped to coach his Little League baseball team, or how we always talked as a family that everyone was a part of Dad's work. His friends had fathers who worked at jobs about which the kids knew nothing. He, however, went to youth retreats with me, and every summer our family vacation was connected with a trip to our state or national convention, or to one of the large Conference Centers owned by the Southern Baptist Convention. If anything, Lilly Faye and I had worked diligently to assure our children that they did not have to participate just because they were the pastor's kids. It seemed to us that they really wanted to be part of church and the many activities associated with it.

Nevertheless, to this day I am grieved about the fact that I know there were many times I was too busy for my family. One of the saddest memories I have is of Lilly Faye and the three kids driving away from our house on Saturday mornings, going to the shopping mall while I get in my car to go visiting prospects or others who needed encouragement from the pastor. Until the last ten years of my pastorate, it had always been my practice to leave my house about mid-morning on most Saturdays and not come home until after dark. After all, this was a good day to catch people at home. And if they were at home on Saturday, there was a good chance they would be in town on Sunday and able to attend church. Then, when I did get home, I would study my sermon for two or three hours.

In discussions with Van, God has mercifully revealed many things to me. Some of these understandings have come from the Lord through my insightful son. On one occasion, he said to me, "Dad, you are too hard on yourself. You need to put the past to bed!" The next thing he said to me gave my spirit wings to fly. "I was thinking about how your grandfather, Robert Wisdom, died when Granddad Wisdom was just a couple of years old. Just think about it; your dad had no one to model for him how to be a father. He didn't have a father. When you came along, he was an absent father to you, working on the tugboat and being gone three-fourths of the time. I've heard you say you never remember your dad throwing a ball to you, or taking you to a movie. He didn't even attend your high school graduation or when you graduated from college or the seminary."

"What are you saying, son?" I asked.

"That in my eyes, you have been a father who, given your background, was very intentional about spending time with Carla, Rose, and me." He continued to speak as my heart grew lighter and lighter, "Both Carla and Rose say they never felt you were disinterested in them or the things they were involved in. Of course you have acknowledged you could have done a better job, but what father or mother doesn't feel the same way about their parenting?" Obviously, his comments made me feel much better.

Yet, the last day of Van's life, when he was still alert, I felt I had to ask him one last time to forgive me for not being a better father. He looked at me for a few minutes, with sadness in his eyes, and simply said, "I forgive you, Dad."

Dear Charles,

It was such a shock to learn yesterday that Van had passed away. Although we never met Van, I want you to know how much Van has impacted our family. We listened to him speak on tape several times and have found such <u>encouragement</u> and <u>hope</u> through his messages! Our family has gone through a difficult time this year, and God has used Van to get us successfully through it.

I am quite sure that God will continue to use Van's life and ministry to touch and heal lives for years to come. <u>You raised a fine son, Charles</u> — he has (and is) served Jesus well!

A fellow father

CHAPTER 2—RESTORING THE YEARS

At Van's memorial service, the verse of scripture I used in the sermon was Joel 2:25.
"I will restore the years the locusts have eaten."
This is a reference to the national disaster experienced by the people of Judah when they had turned their hearts away from God. Joel's message was twofold. One: the people must repent and turn back to God in the face of what they had experienced (invasion of locusts) and in light of the pending *day of the Lord* that had the potential to be much more devastating. Two: there was, however, hope for those who would return in faith to God. The prophet sought to comfort the people with a message of future salvation and blessing. God would stay His hand in further judgment and, at the same time, restore that which had been destroyed by the locusts.

The heart of the message was that God had, in fact, "restored the years the locusts had eaten" in our son's life. He returned to fellowship with his Lord and, in addition, God had opened great doors of opportunity to share his story and have an important role in healing the lives of many others. His family and close friends were constantly amazed at the almost miraculous ways God worked through him.

Am I like many parents who think their children are truly exceptional? Am I, now that he has died, making Van to be someone greater than he was in real life? It is possible; I am aware that grief can erase bad memories and cause one to think of only the good things. Time will tell.

Nonetheless, I am convinced God gave Van unusual abilities. These traits could have produced an even more exceptional life if he had lived. It is probably a "dad thing," but I had dreams of the two of us ministering side by side for years to come. "Surely," I say to myself, "opportunities would have grown much more if Van had lived." However, as the great lion Aslan said to Lucy, "No one is ever told what would have happened."[1]

Van did some great things before he came face to face with the Lord. However, the positives were neutralized in the sense that they were offset by his destructive choices. Part of his life was "devoured by locusts."

In early 1996, Van moved in with Lilly Faye and me so he could save money to buy a house. He had a good job and his health was robust. He worked out almost every day at a health club, and he was feeling cautiously confident about his future. Lilly Faye and I were happy to have him back home. Our loss of some freedom around the house (the empty nest is no longer empty) was worth the price. We were concerned about his health and, mostly, his spiritual condition.

When he moved in, the challenge was to treat him as the adult he was, yet exercise the responsibility we felt to maintain a certain level of control on hours he came and went, etc. With that in mind, I suggested we sign a "covenant" and he readily agreed. I gave him the following memo:

Van,

Mom and I are very happy to have you move in with us for the next few months while you save money to buy a house. We really hope it works out well for you. However, we know we could easily get on each other's nerves unless we have some mutually agreed-on guidelines. Therefore, would you do the following:

(1). Look over the issues we want you to be aware of as you move in with us. Are they reasonable? Are any clarifications needed?

What do we need to discuss in order to be clear about the letter and spirit of our requests?

(2) Would you make your own list of things Mom and I can do to help make our time with each other as positive as possible?

PLEASE CONSIDER DOING THE FOLLOWING:

1. Do not stay out late at night, at least not without telling us about it beforehand. If you do find yourself staying out after midnight, please call and let us know. Believe it or not, we don't sleep well when you are out late even though we know you are an adult and can take care of yourself.

2. You will need to go to church while you live with us. We'd love that to be First Baptist of Katy, but if you prefer going elsewhere, that will be okay with us. I just can't see us going off to church on Sunday mornings and you being in bed. It will be respectful of you to be sensitive to us on this issue.

3. I am asking the following of you. Please keep your room picked up and don't expect Mom to do this for you. She would gladly do so. However, treat her as though you were a guest in a stranger's house; you would keep things picked up out of courtesy. Do that here also, please.

We can talk about other things that will come up; communication will be important. Thankfully, I can see that already happening since you've moved in with us. We're overjoyed to have these opportunities to be more often with you.

We love you mucho!
Dad and Mom

Van was happy with the suggestions and gladly complied. As I indicated in the memo, open communication was occurring more frequently. Both parties had vested interest in seeing things run smoothly. That is not to say, however, that he was openly embracing a fresh relationship with Christ. That was not happening, at least not outwardly. Lilly Faye and I had a deep burden in our hearts for the clear return of Van to an intimate relationship with Christ. I tried hard not to preach at him, and failed many times.

Five years before he died, two things happened to lead him back to his earlier commitment to the Lord. The First Baptist Church of Katy was host to a prayer conference led by T.W. Hunt, a former professor of mine from years earlier when he taught at Southwestern Baptist Seminary. God used T.W. in a remarkable way to touch the heart of our son.

(Some six or seven years earlier, I was attending a conference in North Carolina at an encampment where T. W. Hunt was one of the feature speakers. He and I had a chance to visit and one afternoon he asked me, "Charlie, what prayer needs do you have? What is going on in your life that needs prayer support?" I told him, without giving details, that Lilly Faye and I were really concerned about the decisions our son was making and how he had, at least in our understanding, walked away from the Lord. So I asked him to pray for Van. He told me he would pray for Van regularly. After that, every time I saw T. W. at a conference or convention, he would ask, "How is Van doing?" Here was a spiritual giant, traveling and ministering around the world, and he remembered my son's name and would assure me he was praying for Van. I knew in my heart that something good was going to come from that.)

When the prayer conference ended, T. W. again asked me about Van. I told him Van was having some health issues, and seemed more open to the Lord. T.W. volunteered to go home with Lilly Faye and me and visit with him. We agreed, a little apprehensive that it would appear as though we were ganging up on him.

T.W. handled things with great expertise. After visiting for fifteen minutes or so, he said, "Van, is there some place you and I can go to visit?" Lilly Faye and I immediately got up and walked out of the room as Van said, "Sure, there is a room at the back of the house; let's go there." Some time later, Van and T.W. walked back into the kitchen area where we were. Van's eyes were red; he had been crying. However, he was also smiling as T.W. said, "Van and

I have been praying and he assures me the time has come for him to retrace his steps to where he left the Lord a few years ago." That was big!!

The second thing that was happening in the midst of all of this was Van's health status. Along about this time, he discovered he had Hodgkin's Disease, cancer of the lymph glands. Since Van's immune system was compromised, he could never get completely on top of the cancer. As I said earlier, he went through a repeating cycle: feeling well—feeling sick—treatment. He was tired of this struggle. What many of us did not know, however, was that there was an inner, spiritual restlessness.

After T.W. had visited, Van was uncertain of his next steps. He found greater joy in being back at church and began to develop friendships with several of the young adults. When he and I would talk, I would encourage him to tell his story. A part of him wanted to do that, but his shame and sense of guilt held him back.

During this time, Van became sick again and had a fever so high he had to be hospitalized. He called me and said, "Dad, I think I have come to terms with what the Lord wants me to do. When you come to the hospital later today, would you bring a tape recorder with you?"

When I arrived at his room in the hospital, he told me he wanted to tape a brief testimony relating some of his story. It turned out to be a six-minute tape in which he told of his time of spiritual rebellion, his homosexual behavior resulting in having the HIV virus, and his eagerness to find help in doing the right thing.

That brief tape was profound in its impact! Observations from the many who heard it said it had grabbed their attention. One person remarked, "It went straight to my heart."

With Van's permission and input, Lilly Faye and I decided the time had come to open the dark door of family secrecy. We invited twenty-five close friends who were also church members to our house. After they had listened to the tape, we said, "We need two things from you. One is to ask you to pray for Van and also for us. He needs healing and we need discernment. The second is to seek your advice. We intend to help Van all we can. What is your counsel to us? Should we continue as pastor of the church? What will our church, as well as the entire community, think of this? What is the Lord impressing on your hearts to say to us?"

First one and then another spoke up to offer encouragement. The outpouring of concern overwhelmed us. Some wept. Almost everyone embraced us and gave assurances of continued love and support. Their message was clear and strong: "Tell Van to go forward with his intentions and let us stand by your side through it all." That night was the most liberating one we had experienced in three or four years.

There was no holding back now. We immediately set up a second meeting with another twenty-five people at the home of one of the couples present at the first night. Again, we played the tape, made the appeal for prayer support and suggestions, and were strongly supported by every person present.

The third and fourth meetings were held the following week with another great supportive response. By then, we were inviting other people who had been significant in our lives and/or ministry as well as church members.

(The reader needs to remember that Satan and the forces of darkness love secrets that have the potential to hurt once they are known. Satan does not want us to share openly with others. Transparency and humility of heart flies in the face of his lies that it is better to give the impression that all is well with us. "Be prideful; don't show weaknesses or failures," is what He whispers in our ears.

God admonishes us, however, to "Confess your sins to each other and pray for each other so that you may be healed."[2] How and when this is done, of course, is very important. The confessor of notable sin will want to do this in consultation with others who are wise and can be trusted.)

King David of Israel committed adultery and tried to cover it with murder.[3] After facing his sin and acknowledging it, his testimony was "Before I confessed my sins, my bones felt limp, and I groaned all day long. Night and day your hand weighed heavily on me, and my strength was gone as in the summer heat. So I confessed my sins and told them all to you. I said, 'I'll tell the Lord each one of my sins.' Then you forgave me and took away my guilt. You put songs in my heart."[4]

I had decided there was another group of people I wanted to talk to before we went any further: the pastors of Katy. I sent a written invitation to every pastor I knew in Katy to attend a meeting, indicating that I had something of extreme importance to tell them. I sought to get a response by saying, "There is a story that will be made public in Katy soon and I want you to hear all about it first from me." About thirty pastors of every denomination in the city came to that meeting. I played the tape and again asked for prayers and counsel. Their support was wonderful! Not only had a major load been lifted off my shoulders, but also I felt a bonding with the men and women present. It was so encouraging!

We played the tape and told our story to the senior adults of the church. Lilly Faye made an insightful comment to them: "You may be the most difficult group for us to talk with, because many of you are the ages our parents would be if they were still alive. To talk with you is a little like sharing this painful information with them." We were afraid of how these older people would respond. That fear melted when, many of them in tears, fell on us with hugs, kisses, and reassurances that they understood, loved us, and would pray for Van. Later that morning, one dear lady sobbed as she told us about a grandson who was involved in homosexual behavior.

An important observation about every one of these seven encounters: at least two or three people in every group with whom we shared, including the pastors, spoke with us about a child, brother or sister, or themselves who struggled with some aspect of sexual brokenness. More than one story of HIV status also surfaced. It was like giving people permission to reveal their burdens when they learned of our own. Just a few days after Van had spoken to the entire church, a member of our congregation came to tell me of the heavy burden she and her husband carried. Her daughter had become pregnant at college that year. She said, "I'm sorry, Pastor, for the heartache you and your wife must bear. Yet learning about this situation in your family gave me the courage to come and ask for your prayers and counsel." We were reminded that God can use the life story of a person to set others free as well.

The last group to whom we spoke was the deacon body of the church. While many of them had been present at one of the gatherings of twenty-five, I had specifically waited until the last to talk with the deacons and yokefellows. The night of that meeting, many of our friends unexpectedly showed up to offer their support to us. In addition to the deacons and yokefellows, we had also invited the mayor of the city and his wife. They are active members of the Methodist church and our good friends. Also present were wives of the deacons and yokefellows.

After they had listened to the tape, I said to these church and community leaders, "We need your prayers and support. However, if you think my family or I will hurt our church because of our story, we will offer our resignation if you deem it wise. We will step out into the hall and give you freedom to talk among yourselves; call us in when you are ready."

We visited in the hall with friends for about fifteen minutes before the deacon chairman asked us to come back into the room. When we walked in, every person in the room stood and began to applaud. Many tears were shed. The chairman gave us their decision: "We feel that God is using all of this to bless the Wisdom family and to do something special in our church. Maybe the revival we have been praying for will come to both the church and the community of Katy as well. Our request is to ask Van to share his story with the entire church. To show our support, every deacon and yokefellow in this room will stand behind him on the stage as an indication to him and to the church of our support." (A few years later, Van was invited to join the deacon body. He was honored by the invitation, but declined because of failing health.)

The church was packed the night of Van's testimony. I had strongly urged our membership to be present because of the importance of what would happen on that particular night. Of course, many in the church and community had already heard the story, as they had been in one of the seven group meetings we had earlier. Actually, the story had spread in several directions. In addition to the many members present, my wife and I had also invited our brothers and sisters, nephews and nieces, as well as pastors and civic leaders from the community. Van had said, "There is no need of holding anything back. The entire world is invited to sit in and listen."

A Voice From Heaven

The entire night was, without doubt to anyone present, a "God thing". After music, Van moved to the pulpit and spoke. (See Chapter 5 "Life Is Not A Dress Rehearsal") In the beginning, he was nervous and acknowledged it to the congregation. He indicated he was very sad that his story was going to disappoint many people, but that he had to be obedient to what God had told him he was to do.

The forty-minute testimony ended with Van saying he was not sure of how much time he had left in this world; his HIV status made him aware each day of the uncertainty of life. But he knew one thing for sure: he knew he would be okay because he had the Lord Jesus in his heart and life. Then he began singing:

"Because He lives, I can face tomorrow.
Because He lives, all fear is gone.
Because I know He holds the future.
And life is worth the living, just because He lives."[5]

When he finished, the entire congregation stood and applauded for five minutes. The majority of persons present were weeping and clapping at the same time. When I asked staff members to stand at the front of the sanctuary to pray with any who had need, at least a hundred people came forward. Van was inundated with those who wanted to thank him, ask prayer for someone, or just express love for him. It was an hour before the last person had a chance to speak to him, but they remained.

Because of that night's testimony, Van was immediately drawn into a daily routine of having someone call him to meet for counsel or other reasons. One man invited him to lunch and wept as he told of his youth and how he had sold his body to make money for drugs. Another who was now happily married with several children told of having the HIV virus, but lived with shame because of the things he had done when he was single, and the resulting sexually transmitted disease he had acquired.

Requests to see me also increased as people in the church and community, as well as from around the state, found freedom to share the heavy burdens of their lives and seek help.

Since there had been several pastors in the audience the night of the testimony, Van began to receive invitations to speak at churches around the area. He spoke at Sunday morning services and with youth groups in the church. Several denominations were involved. He also spoke to groups of churches that met for conferences or conventions. Because of the growing counseling appointments requested of him at our church, the Executive Pastor recommended that Van serve on the staff. The Personnel Committee agreed. It was a part-time position with a very small stipend, but he loved it so much and it grew so fast, he spent most days and many evenings meeting and praying with those who came. As a result, he began to work on a Master's Degree in Christian Psychology and Counseling at Houston Baptist University.

Van was offered a fulltime position on staff at the church. He declined that offer, but continued to give biblical counseling and, at the same time, to develop a support group ministry. *New Beginnings* was born from that invitation. During the four years he led this weekly gathering, *New Beginnings* ministered to over three hundred people.

Van and I were invited to share a Father-Son testimony at the annual convention of Exodus International when it met in London the summer of 1999. In breakout sessions and small group counseling, we told our story of how things had developed in our lives from the perspective of father-son. We explained how we had taken our story to a theologically conservative church and the overwhelmingly positive response it received from everyone. We told of how God had used people and circumstances to bring healing to us individually and collectively. We quoted Joseph's words to his brothers when they feared for their lives after having sold him into Egyptian slavery. "You intended to harm me, but God intended it for good to accomplish what is now being done..."[6] We shared with them the unfolding opportunities for Van to help others who wanted to find freedom from homosexuality through Christ-centered counseling and Christian support groups. Lilly Faye and I were able to recount how God was giving us opportunities to comfort and counsel parents (some of whom are in the ministry) of children with sexual abuse or same-sex attraction issues.

We would review the day's activities, and his discernment in interpreting those events, even the way he expressed himself, spoke powerfully to me.

Many of those late-night discussions revolved around issues at church. Once, I remember having a difficult time with one of the leaders in the congregation. As we talked about the situation, he gave me wise counsel on how to respond. In our discussion, we formulated a three-step plan for dealing with this specific problem that was bearing down on me. I was elated!! It made lots of sense and I thought, "This is going to be ok; I feel good about the outcome and how I can deal with this difficult situation!"

Then, in a gentle and soft voice he said, "Dad, have you thought about *your* contribution to the problems between you and him?"

I wanted to be a little defensive, but the lack of accusation in his voice and demeanor disarmed me. I searched for a reply as he continued, "I could be wrong, but it seems you have brought some of this problem on yourself." He mentioned how I had dropped a particular ministry idea in this man's lap without giving him any time to think about it. When the member questioned why we needed to do the particular thing I was recommending, I subtly accused him of not supporting my leadership. Things had escalated from there. Van had picked up on all of that and knew I had to be aware of it if there was to be genuine reconciliation between this man and me. As soon as I saw things from Van's viewpoint, I knew we had to fine-tune that reconciliation plan. I was again reminded that God had turned my son into my counselor!

The way God used Van to help people with personal issues was wonderful. Some of the stories were interesting in other ways as well. For instance, I once invited a psychiatrist to speak to our congregation about bi-polar illnesses. We were facing a situation in the church with one of our staff members who was diagnosed with this condition and felt we needed this doctor to explain to our membership how we could best respond to the staff member, particularly when he was experiencing an episode of behavior related to his illness.

The psychiatrist and I were seated on the front row in the auditorium, visiting and waiting for the service to begin. As we sat there,

While in London for the conference, we met a team of television personalities who were from the United States. Their purpose in being at the conference was to interview and tape sessions with persons who had inspirational stories to tell. The television market for this particular group was the Southeast region of the United States. While there, we were fortunate to be interviewed. Later, we learned that particular television presentation was widely broadcast with a great deal of favorable response. There has been follow-up contact with me since that time. It is but one more reason I am grateful to God for the way He has used Van's story to touch others.

Van also had the opportunity to tell his story of God's grace and restoring love to a group who toured Israel in the winter of 2000. Included in the group were Lilly Faye, our daughter Carla Faye Robinson, and me. When we visited Gordon's Tomb, one of the sites believed to be the place where Jesus was buried after his crucifixion, we had a brief worship service. Before observing The Lord's Supper, Van spoke to the group and shared his story. He wept. We all wept. It was one of the most moving experiences I have ever had. In that sacred spot, we were able to hear again of the wonderful grace and restoring love of our Lord Jesus Christ. The reminder that Christ had come to earth to die as God's sacrificial lamb in order to set us free from sin's captivity was powerfully demonstrated that day!

HOUSTON BAPTIST UNIVERSITY

It became clear to Van that his destiny was to help people! After his story became community-wide property, most of his days were spent talking with and/or counseling people who wanted more and more of his attention. It seemed to me that he became a magnet; people were drawn to him. When we went out to eat, or to a movie, he would be approached by people both known and unknown to him. I remember wondering if he had always had this magnetic draw about him, and I was just now opening my eyes to his people skills. Honestly, I think it was that, but more. There was spiritual energy released in Van that had to come from the Lord. It was as though great spiritual potential in him for years surfaced overnight! We began a nightly routine when I arrived home from the office.

a well-known man in our community came over to talk with me. It turned out he was eager to thank me for having Van as leader of the *New Beginnings* ministry and to give me a progress report on how well his daughter was doing. This very capable and well-educated young lady had struggled with issues in her life since high school. Van had met with this young lady on several occasions, counseled and prayed with her and through this she had experienced a spiritual re-birth. As a result, she had found a more stable life and was very profitably employed. According to this beaming dad, she was happier than she had been in a long, long time.

While thanking me for Van's ministry in the church and especially in his daughter's life, he said, "You know, Pastor, my wife and I have taken this girl to more psychiatrists and psychologists than we can count. Van has helped her more in the last six months than all those people put together!" (Seeing this coming, I stood immediately and tried to gently move him a bit further away, hoping all the time the good doctor had not overheard his remarks. If she had, she graciously looked the other way and never made comment about it...nor did I!)

As I mentioned, Van enrolled at Houston Baptist University and worked toward a Master's Degree in Christian Psychology and Counseling. He loved it! And he did well; he made straight A's in every course he took. Lacking just one class to get his degree when he died, the President of the University, Dr. E. D. Hodo, received permission from the faculty and administration of the university to confer the degree posthumously. Dr. Hodo came to the memorial service and presented Lilly Faye and me with his degree.

Van died the last day of February in 2002. In May of that year, I was invited to deliver the graduation message at Houston Baptist University commencement. The title of the sermon was "He being Dead, Yet Speaks" from Hebrews 11:4. (see Chapter 8)

In spite of his death, Van's story is gaining momentum. Lilly Faye and I counsel people who struggle with same-sex attraction. We've spoken to over one hundred parents whose kids are involved in this lifestyle. We have had the opportunity to tell his and our story on many other occasions. The privilege of facilitating support groups has been given to us as well. We participate in *Compassionate*

Friends and offer our encouragement to parents whose child has died. Meanwhile, over five hundred copies of Van's testimony on tape or CD have been distributed. On the anniversary of his death these past four years, we have shown videos of Van's life and testimony at the churches I serve.

Truly, God fully restored the years the locusts devoured in Van's life and in the Wisdom family.

Dear Uncle Charlie and Aunt Lilly Faye,
It's hard to believe that it has been a month now since Van has gone. The world just isn't the same. Van was such a special and unique person. You two raised a wonderful man. One of the messages that Van was able to convey so well is God's faithfulness to forgive and restore.
A.J.

Dear Charlie and Lilly Faye,
I know how much you love your children. Last year you gave me a tape of Van's testimony. I listened and was greatly moved. I played it for my teenage grandchildren and others. They were moved to tears. Surely God used, and will continue to use, his testimony in a powerful way.
B.R.R.

CHAPTER 3 — THE ROAD BACK HOME

Overcoming Same-Sex Attraction

How did Van overcome his attraction to homosexuality? During our many conversations on related subjects, and listening to him speak or give a testimony, I believe he would answer it was both a *decision* and a *process*.

When he made the decision to tell his story to the world in the context of regret and repentance, he turned his back on all the arguments he had embraced for living with the misery he was experiencing. The Christian would say it is like being "born again."[1]

However, Van would emphatically state the need of growth in many areas of one's life: in understanding what has happened to cause the struggle, in rebuilding wholesome relationships, especially with men, and in moving from living in shadows and darkness to the light of honesty and transparency. In addition, there is the need of networking with family, friends, and others who can help keep one accountable. Most of all, for the Christian, the need of continual growth in knowledge of and love for Jesus Christ is crucial.

I'm getting ahead of myself in this explanation. Let me begin with what those wiser and more knowledgeable than I teach are the *causes* of same-sex attraction.

FALSE EXPLANATIONS

1. Biological.

A growing number of people in American society, strongly influenced by liberal media and the activism of entertainment personalities, (particularly those in movies and television) believe one is biologically linked to homosexuality. Their message is *homosexuals are born that way.* Just as some people have blue eyes while other's eyes are brown, some people are born heterosexual and others are born homosexual.

The results of this growing misunderstanding? Proponents of this view preach American society must abandon its puritanical and obsolete ideas about human sexuality and embrace as normal behavior those who choose same-sex lifestyles. Most of these people would have us redefine "family" as anyone who loves another and chooses to live with that person or persons.

2. Choice.

It is obvious to most people in western society that traditional explanations for the meaning of life have radically changed the past fifty-plus years. The Judeo-Christian worldview of human sexuality, viz. sex is for married adults who are in a lifetime commitment, has been rejected in a Post-Christian world. This has given birth to a variety of unhealthy lifestyles such as living together without the benefit of marriage, divorce, and multiple marriages, and *the freedom, and in some cases encouragement, to choose non-traditional approaches to sexual fulfillment.* Choosing to engage in same-sex activity, for both homosexual and heterosexual persons, is applauded in some circles. A recent television talk show spoke of youth who are demonstrating their support of homosexuals by engaging in same-sex activity even though they are heterosexuals. "Different strokes for different folks," we are told. "If it doesn't hurt you or others in any way, why be against it? The progressive way is to embrace any style of giving and receiving sexual fulfillment. If you don't want it, fine. Just don't be narrow and deny it to those who do choose homosexuality."

Van once told me that most homosexuals, given the chance, would never choose a lifestyle that would alienate them from some of their family or portions of society. In that sense, he would say, choosing to arbitrarily embrace homosexuality is not attractive at all. The point is, there are factors that promote homosexuality in those who are attracted to it. These factors, as explained below, are often thrust on a person who might not otherwise embrace the same-sex life style.

JUDEO-CHRISTIAN EXPLANATIONS

Christians who believe the Bible is the supernatural word of God also believe one can learn the truth about human nature and why we live as we do.

I am indebted to Dr. T.W. Hunt for the following information that embodies, in embryo form, both *cause* and *cure* of homosexuality.[2]

1. Creation demonstrates the original intention of God for our well-being. He created the anatomy of the male for the female and vice versa. He did not create the anatomy of one sex for the same sex. Thus, going back to the very beginning of life on earth, we learn quickly that God created Adam and Eve by design. Sexual activity for procreation and mutual joy was in the mind of God. Humans are "out-of-sync" with fundamental truth when this law of creation is broken.

2. However, the current anti-Judeo-Christian ambience in much of the western world reduces all behavior to physical causes. Thus, there are genetic, chemical, biological or other explanations for behavior and not a "right or wrong" reason. This results in failing to see the destructiveness in homosexuality and denies the need of correction.

Absolutes about sexual behavior are *absolutely discarded*. The possibility of the spiritual as a logical cause or solution of anything is denied. It is not in the realm of this worldview that the spiritual could possibly transform or change someone's sexual orientation and/or behavior.

3. Unfortunately, there is in media and academia a very active movement to stifle the conscience. Westerners are urged to adopt "openness" toward behavior that had previously been seen as unnatural. The sad result is that American society, along with other parts of the world, is suffering the results of a devastating blindness to reality as God intended it to be. To make matters worse, many never make the connection between choosing to engage in destructive behavior and what happens as a consequence.

Psychiatrist Dr. Jeffrey Satinover, professor at Yale and Harvard, has authored what the Congressional Record submits to be "The best book on homosexuality written in our lifetime."[3] Satinover agrees with T.W. Hunt's theological perspective, though he approaches the subject from what he identifies as the "bio-psycho-social" model. Three propositions, according to Dr. Satinover, are erroneously presented as being the correct approach to understanding homosexuality. Conventional wisdom asserts:

1. First, as a matter of *biology*, homosexuality is an innate, genetically determined aspect of the human body.
2. Second, as a matter of *psychology*, homosexuality is irreversible. Indeed, the attempt to reverse it requires so profound a denial of self that it is said to cause the widely acknowledged, higher- than-average mental problems among homosexuals, such as depression, suicide, alcohol and drug abuse.
3. Third, as a matter of *sociology*, homosexuality is normal, akin to other social categories such as sex and race.

Dr. Satinover's view is the opposite:
1. Homosexuality is not innate, but a choice.[4]
2. Homosexuality is reversible.[5]
3. Homosexuality is not normal, but an illness or perversion of nature.[6]

Let's return to Van's situation. Here are the reasons he believed and taught that he chose to become involved in homosexual activities.

SEXUAL ABUSE

When he was seven or eight years of age, Van was abused by a teenage boy who was in a youth group I led while serving as a missionary in Mexico. (The boy was an American, not a Mexican.) Tragically, when we later lived in San Antonio, an adult man again sexually abused Van. Though he never would give details or mention names to us, Van related to me that he had entered intensive counseling as a young adult in order to deal with the trauma of those experiences. This came after his decision to abandon the same-sex behavior lifestyle. Whereas Van had tried to convince himself earlier that he was "born gay," he later determined that his abuse as a child had greatly contributed to his sexual identity confusion.

Dr. David Finkelhor confirms this in an account presented by the *National Association For Research and Therapy on Homosexuals.* "Some of the consequences of Childhood seduction include confusion about sexual identity and sexual norm, and an inability to differentiate sex from love."[5]

Many homosexuals give accounts of having been sexually abused as small children. I've heard different statistics correlating that relationship, ranging from 37%[6] to much higher percentages linking the number of male homosexuals who were abused as children. In 2003, my wife and I attended the National Conference of *Exodus International, USA* in Orlando, Florida. I took the President, Alan Chambers, to lunch one day and asked him, "I've read that maybe as high as 80% or more of male homosexuals were sexually abused as children. Do you know if that is correct?" Alan replied, "I'm not sure about that, but I know that more than 90% of the registrants at our conference this year report having been sexually abused as children."[7] (In January of 2006, I heard Alan and his wife on a radio talk show. He had come to believe, he said, that 98% of male homosexuals were sexually abused when they were children.)

FATHER-SON BONDING

I will always be burdened with the thought that I contributed to Van's lack of male identity. When the father and young son fail to bond emotionally, mixed with additional factors that exaggerate this sad reality, the boy may look to men for affirmation. This can easily lead to sexual activity in later years.

Dr. Satinover touches on this aspect of same-sex attraction. "For whatever reason, he recalls a painful 'mismatch' between what he needed and longed for and what his father offered him."[8]

Was I too busy to spend time with Van? Did I fail to listen to him, or give him unspoken messages that I did not want to relate to him? Could I have showered too much love on his older sister and lead him to decide I did not love him the way I loved her? I honestly do not know the answers to these questions. He and I talked about them often in our heart-to-heart discussions and especially when we attended counseling together. Van was eager to reassure me, but I suffered much in my heart over this issue for some time. I still find it difficult to write about it.

A FUN-LOVING GUY

As indicated earlier, Van loved to have fun. He delighted in being with people and was almost always the life of the party. When he left home for college, his intense interest and skills in gymnastics resulted in being elected a yell leader at the university. There, he became friends with two young men who, like him, had male identity issues. Because he never told me the details of how and when he became involved, I do not know exactly the sequence of things. Yet, during this time, Van began to engage in homosexual activities. Meanwhile, they talked with him about the "gay gene" and convinced him he was indeed a homosexual and he might as well embrace it. Initially, he said, he felt relieved when he decided that he did not have a problem; it was a problem of society ("homophobia") that caused him and his newfound friends grief.

Homosexuals, generally, are famous for being "party animals." Once you are inducted into this "fraternity," you will have more opportunities to attend socials, parties, gatherings, etc. than you can possibly keep up with. All of this, of course, reinforces your newly embraced identity and, at the same time, provides a network of people with whom you establish a new "family."

THE WAKE-UP CALL!!

Once we learned about Van's involvement in homosexuality, Lilly Faye, his sisters, and I prayed fervently for him. We told him so frequently. We never parted, no matter how brief a period we might be separated, but that we said, "We love you and are praying for you." I did not give details, but often asked friends and others to pray for him. I called television and radio ministries where an appeal would be made for listeners to share prayer requests. I asked them to pray for my son who was out of fellowship with the Lord.

Soon after we learned about Van's involvement with homosexuality, he wrote all of us saying, "I am gay and will move to Europe. I do not want to hurt any of you. I love you all very much. I will never see you again. Please forgive me." We were devastated!! Lilly Faye and I were unable to sleep and we constantly discussed our options. How could we intervene? What could we do to force an adult child to abandon what he considered to be his true destiny? I admit my faith was small and we were on the brink of despair.

I was convinced my ministry was over, that I had failed so completely as a father that I did not merit the privilege of being a pastor. We had decided the thing to do was to move to another city and begin life over. Yet, we felt no peace in our hearts about that decision. We just couldn't muster emotional strength to pull up stakes and move on.

A few months later, a pastor friend called and invited me to breakfast with one of his staff members and a visiting Bible teacher, Jack Taylor. I had met Jack when we were pastors together in San Antonio. I admired him greatly and jumped at the chance to visit with him again. However, during the breakfast, I had to fight to keep back tears. My mind was focused on Van and the burden that was on my heart.

A Voice From Heaven

After breakfast, I asked Jack if I could see him for a few minutes. We went to his room and I immediately blurted out, "Jack, I have just learned the past few months that my son is homosexual!! My wife and I are about to die. We just don't know what to do or how to respond. We think we need to resign the ministry and move away." By now, I was weeping.

Jack Taylor was the voice of God to me! He said, "Charles, Satan has won a victory in Van's life. Don't let him intimidate you into running away! Stand up to him! God promises us that if we resist the devil, he will flee from us."[9]

His next words went deep into my heart: "Your son is not a homosexual." I first thought I had misunderstood him. Then, I thought, "Does he know Van? Is there some information I do not know about? Is that the reason I was invited to this breakfast?"

He continued, "He may have foolishly engaged in homosexual activities, but he is not a homosexual." To this day, I do not know why he said that; I just know it went deeply into my very soul and a sense of peace swept over me. It was truly a "God thing!"

He proceeded to tell me about a young man to whom he had ministered in Fort Worth. This boy had struggled with same-sex temptations. He had talked and prayed with the young man, had recommended him to Christian counseling, and the young fellow was doing very well. He was with a group of other Christian young men who were holding him accountable and encouraging him on a daily basis.

I listened only partially, because the atmosphere in the room was almost mystical: *I felt the Lord had sent me a message that Van was okay.*

We prayed together and I eagerly ran to a phone in the lobby. I couldn't wait to call Lilly Faye! As overwhelmed as I was, I had to tell her what I had just heard and that things were going to be okay. I knew the Lord was going to lead us to victory in this situation, and that our son would be restored to God and to the family! I also told Van the next time I saw him that I had received an assurance from the Lord that things would work out fine. He said, "I hope so," with less enthusiasm than I was feeling.

Things were happening fast. Lilly Faye and I found new hope. Our prayers increased in number and fervency and we began to contact friends, far and wide, to pray for our son. However, the climax of all of this encouraging activity had an initial negative impact: Van was diagnosed with Hodgkin's Disease. This came about a year after it was discovered he was HIV positive. The first thing he asked his doctor was, "Am I with cancer because of my HIV status?" The doctor told him there was a good chance he would have contracted the disease even if he had not been HIV positive. When we left the medical office, Van wept in the car. He told us, "The guilt I have about my destructive choices would be even greater if I knew I had brought this on myself."

However, this is the very instrument God used to bring Van full circle. Hodgkin's Disease is common in young adults with the majority of them entering remission. When it was announced in our church with requests that the people pray for Van, a young man who was present that Sunday called to encourage me. He said, "Pastor, I know you and Mrs. Wisdom are worried about your son. However, I had the same illness and am doing wonderfully well. It is easily controlled." I appreciated his encouragement, but I thought to myself, "However, your immune system is much stronger than is Van's!"

The health events were cyclical: he would do well for six months or so, then have a flare up with the cancer and have to go back to chemotherapy. Then, he would get better and try to put his condition out of his mind, only to have a recurring bout with the disease again. That was Van's life for a few years, but all the time he was inching his way back to the Lord (attending church frequently and going to counseling with me, openly discussing the many facets of his choices).

Van became very ill on one occasion (six years before he died), and he called me to his hospital room to say that he was ready to give up his internal struggle against God, acknowledge his sin and wanting to reconnect with the Lord. That started the heaven-directed process of publicly announcing his situation and intentions of renewing his relationship with God!

COUNSELING AND MUTUAL SUPPORT

Van would insist that a major reason he was able to make the difficult break with same-sex philosophy and behavior was because of the people he connected with in the following years. He continued in counseling for a long time with Michael Newman. Michael had spent many years in homosexuality and had found freedom in Christ. This led to establishing a ministry to persons who, either they or their family, struggled with homosexuality. He is very knowledgeable and lent strong support to Van and each of us. Van actually worked with Michael at various times in offering counsel to families with this concern.

Additionally, Van was part of support groups established by Mr. Newman. These gatherings of persons with same-sex attractions were of tremendous benefit to Van. He was learning how others had found help with their situations. He heard testimonies of victories and disappointments. He was given books to read, tapes to listen to, and he devoured all of this information with tremendous interest.

This led to Van connecting with other ministries that reached out to homosexuals. Some he participated in via correspondence and others he traveled to in order to attend. Meanwhile, he was being inundated with requests for help from individuals or families caught up in this devastating condition. (He was also severely criticized by some of the homosexual community. Strangely, those attacks backfired because of the faulty messages given to him and the hate accompanying them. Van always replied, "If you want to chose a life of homosexuality, you may do so. But don't attack others or me because we want to find freedom from it!")

One of the organizations that helped Van, as well as Lilly Faye and me, is Exodus International.[10] We attended one international (London) and three national conventions, and were overwhelmed by the presence and testimonies of thousands of young adults who had overcome homosexuality or who were desperately searching for help. Medical personnel, psychiatrists and psychologists, and ministries that are directed by former homosexuals, offered seminars, presentations, testimonies, case studies, and a mass of help to those who want to learn of, and experience, freedom from homosexuality.

(I have referred to this ministry that coordinates literally hundreds of similar ministries around the world as "America's best kept secret." In the midst of overwhelming discussions in American society about homosexuality, one hears very little from the media about this organization!!)

COMPLETE HEALING

Alan Chamber, President of Exodus International, was asked on a Christian radio talk-show: "Can the person who has struggled with same-sex issues, once he or she has found freedom in Christ and is in some kind of healthy, on-going accountability relationship, be completely healed in the sense they never have same-sex attractions again?" Mr. Chamber's answer was there are thousands of men and women who, once they turn from homosexuality to Jesus Christ and find a network of family and friends who pray for them and encourage them, do find complete healing! Scores of people who once engaged in homosexual activity are now happily married with children and grandchildren with 10, 20, 30, and 40 years of same-sex resistance. Others, Alan said, are like people who have a drug addiction and struggle tremendously in the beginning. The emotional bondage from which many homosexuals have to be freed can return to tempt them again and again. For instance, a man or woman who has had an affair, who repents and never again crosses that line, may yet have times of temptation with which to deal.

Lastly, unfortunately, some fall away and return to old patterns of behavior. It is imperative that a Christian who has been victimized by any destructive behavior makes every effort to grow stronger in the Lord. The bottom line is, each of us must continue to pray, serve Christ faithfully, all the while realizing we are engaged in a fearsome spiritual war as long as we are in this world.[11]

This was Van's viewpoint as well, and he frequently warned himself and those with whom he counseled not to think "I've got it made now; no more troubles in that realm of my life." He led the *New Beginnings* ministry at his church and constantly brought in speakers to teach or give testimony of how easy it is to, as he said, "Get out of the marsh, stand on the Solid Rock, only to slip back into it again." Nevertheless, victory over homosexuality is a reality in the lives of thousands of people who have turned to God and found His forgiveness and new life.

For several reasons, I wish Van could have lived many more years. I would love to have continued my years of public ministry with him at my side. I could see he was already focusing on issues of "How do we grow up in Jesus Christ? How do I find greater strength, and how can I help others become more solid in their new life?"

Dear Dr. and Mrs. Wisdom,

I am praying for you. Even though I was only able to see Van at Exodus Conferences, I was so blessed by him. His joy was contagious! I always felt like we were kindred spirits in a way—both hyper, smiling, dancers, same issues, and of course, both Christians. I remember (very clearly) meeting Van for the first time in Seattle. He showed me some of his cheer moves and then seized the dance floor at the hotel as his own!! What a joyful heart! His testimony and the <u>bravery</u> he showed inspires me greatly.
D.H.

Dear Dr. and Mrs. Wisdom,

My heart aches at the loss of your beautiful son and my treasured friend, Van. I'm writing this letter because I want you to know of the impact Van has had in my life. I'm sure you know of the many lives Van has touched and the many he witnessed to and befriended and the many souls he has won over to the Lord, but I want you to know about the work God did in my life through Van. Before I met Van I was lost. I was brought up in a Christian home with loving parents, who although they made mistakes, nonetheless provided love and a godly home.

I recognized Van in one of my classes, that he was from church and we struck up a conversation in class. Van told me about New Beginnings at our church and invited me to go several times until I ran out of excuses. See, I was afraid of rocking my little world that I had put together on my own. I knew if I started taking steps toward

God, getting to know Him and finding Truth and His love, I would have to give Him the reins of my life. That was very scary to me. Van soon became my spiritual counselor and a great friend. We had many rap sessions, many laughs, and many tears. Van ministered to me and God through Van changed my life. I was truly brought to the cross and am saved.

I thank God for His perfect plan and the way he used Van.
S.

CHAPTER 4—JOY AND GRIEF TOGETHER

○○○

In I Peter 1:6 we read, "you greatly rejoice, though now for a little while you may have had to suffer grief..." On the first anniversary of Van's death, I used this passage to describe how grateful our family is for the good things about the way he died.

Charles Dickens' well-read novel <u>A Tale of Two Cities</u> has the famous opening line, "It was the best of times; it was the worst of times."[1] This paradoxical statement fits exactly the way my wife and I felt about the death of our son. After ten years of being HIV positive and five years of having Hodgkin's disease, Van died within six weeks of learning he had a malignant brain tumor. Two weeks later, sitting at my desk and writing feverishly the thoughts that were rushing into my mind, I listed several reasons Van's death was a good death. I feel now, as then, that God visited me. He was saying that, though we were in the depth of grief, we also had reason to celebrate and praise Him for the circumstances surrounding Van's leaving this earth for heaven.

Not too long after I had recorded my thoughts about the many positive aspects surrounding Van's death, our children and grandchildren were visiting us again. We sat down together and I shared with them the thoughts the Lord had placed in my heart. We cried and we thanked God together! We experienced what Paul meant when he said to the Thessalonians, "We do not want you to grieve like those who have no hope..."[2]

Cyrus L. Sulzberger once said, "The manner of death is more important than the death itself."[3] Seventeenth century novelist Henry Fielding wrote, "It is not death, but dying, which is terrible."[4] While one might question portions of the philosophies of these two men, there is a great deal of truth in what they say. <u>How</u> we die is important. I have told my wife and others that I'd love to die the way Van died. The manner in which he passed was such a blessing to us; we want to share it with others for their comfort. May great honor be attributed to our loving God who provides for all our needs, even in death.

Before proceeding with the many positive things about the way Van died, it is imperative to make clear we are not glossing over the deep pain with which our family struggles. We're not trying to take a short cut in our grieving process. We refuse to look the other way, but embrace our grief. At the time of this writing, several months had passed since Van's death. There is still not a day that passes by but I think of him.

Erwin W. Lutzer, pastor of Moody Memorial Church in Chicago, writes in his book <u>One Minute After You Die</u>, "Dying grace does not mean that we will be free from sorrow whether at our own impending death or the death of someone we love. Sorrow and grief are to be expected. If we feel the pain of loneliness when a friend of ours moves from Chicago to Atlanta, why should we not feel genuine grief when a friend leaves for heaven?"[5] The great Reformer John Calvin said, "Death has been destroyed in such a way as to be no longer fatal for Believers, but not in such a way as to cause them no trouble."[6]

To help us deal with our grief, Lilly Faye and I entered counseling with a Christian therapist. Our purpose was to have a wise, spiritually minded person objectively listen to us to ensure that we did not enter into clinical depression.

Another positive step we took to help cope with our deep sorrow was to join Compassionate Friends. This is an international organization of men and women who have lost children to death. There are twenty-five to thirty-five people present at each session. They share about some aspect of the death of their child: how they are coping, what they have learned about themselves, about life, etc. Listening and giving moral support to one another in this kind of environment was very helpful for us.

My point is we put forth an effort to appropriately acknowledge our grief while at the same time opening ourselves to some of the resources God made available. We encouraged one another to remember that "my God shall supply all your needs according to his riches in Christ Jesus,"[7] but we must also collaborate with Him in the healing process.

HOW THEN SHALL WE DIE?

Francis Schaeffer asks Christ-followers, "How then shall we live?"[8] In light of the crucial needs of society and the call of our Savior to respond, how is the sensitive believer to live in this world?

I have another question for us. Since it is determined of God that all humans will leave this earth,[9] "How then shall we *die*?"

The following traits of Van's death impress me as being, at least partially, the answer to this important question.

IN THE LORD

For one, Van died "in the Lord." The Bible teaches, "Blessed are those who die in the Lord."[10] In the Old Testament, a good death was identified by statements such as, "Jacob breathed his last and was gathered to his people."[11] But in the New Testament, the Christ-followers who died serving Him faithfully were identified as those who had "died in the Lord." They died with peace in their hearts because they were in good relationship with Jesus Christ.

Though Van was at peace with God when he died, it was not always that way. As said in the previous chapters, there was a period in his life when he turned his back on the Lord. He once said, in a sermon on the Prodigal Son, "There was a time when I tried to run away from God. I thought only about myself and the plans I had. I sought to put the Lord out of my life and to forget the teachings of my parents. However, I learned through painful experiences that I could never get away from God."

Van always knew there was a good chance he would die young. When he told his story to the entire church on that eventful Sunday night in 1998, he said, "I don't know what the future holds for me. I no longer make long-term goals; that's not an option for me. But I do know whatever happens, it will be okay. I've got God, don't I? Jesus is my Savior and I know that eventually, everything will be all right." He then began to sing, "Because He lives, I can face tomorrow."

Van truly "died in the Lord!" This is the foundational reason for joy in the way our son died. As wonderful as the following attributes of a good death are, they would be less meaningful if Van had died out of fellowship with God!

WITHOUT PAIN

Secondly, Van's death was a good one because he died with very little pain or physical discomfort. The limited amount of suffering he experienced in the last days was controlled by medication, which was never strong enough to send him into a coma until the last two or three hours of his life.

Van was concerned he might face serious pain, but most of all he was worried that he would lose control of his body. When the surgeon talked with us about possible side effects of the brain tumor, he mentioned terrible things like:

.... loss of ability to walk or use his legs.
.... blindness
.... inability to think clearly or speak clearly
.... epileptic-like seizures.

Thankfully none of those ever happened; however, he suffered severe weight loss. He joked that he was getting into shape to be cast in a World War II movie as a suffering Jew in a Nazi concentration camp. There were instances when he had severe physical discomfort. One night, Lilly Faye and I were awakened in the early morning hours with screams coming from his bedroom. Rushing to his side, we found him rolling around his bed saying, "My body is on fire!! I feel like there are shock waves moving up and down my body!!" Thank the Lord this lasted only about three minutes. After he settled down, we talked about the possibility of a stroke. The doctor told us the next day that it was a reaction to the lessening of the steroids in his body—that he was coming off the steroids too quickly and his body reacted. Since it was almost morning, I slept in the easy chair in his room. Lilly Faye took my place around 6:00 A.M. Van slept peacefully until late that morning. Thankfully, he never had that experience again.

Not only was Van in relatively good shape physically and mentally, he also had a fair amount of energy. He would get up and walk into the kitchen three or four times a day to eat and watch television with us. In the last week of his life, he telephoned some of his relatives just to chat with them and to tell them he loved them. He called many of his Baylor friends to do the same. He also enrolled via computer for the last class needed for his master's degree. In fact, the day before he died, he ordered some books for his class, which arrived the day of his funeral.

Dr. Ann Owens, head of the Psychology Department at HBU, related a tender story. She told Lilly Faye and me about a call she received from him one day at school. This took place just a few days before he went to heaven. He talked with her about the last class he needed to complete his degree as well as some other school issues. Then, before saying goodbye, he said, "I love you, Dr. Owen." She said she was overcome with emotion and was momentarily at a loss for words. "I love you too, Van," she replied. That was the last time she ever spoke to him.

Some wonderful things happened during these days when he had extra energy. Van felt so well, he went house shopping with his sister Rose. He originally planned to sit in the car while she pointed out the houses in which she and her husband were interested, but he decided to actually go through some of the houses to look at them in more detail. That was during the weekend before his death the following Wednesday night. He wanted to go to church that Sunday, but Lilly Faye and I were concerned it would be too tiring. Friends and counselees would collect around him and talk for thirty or forty minutes after each service. He always left exhausted, but felt affirmed that he was greatly loved. His last Sunday at church, Van received a spontaneous standing ovation when his presence was mentioned.

That Sunday afternoon after church, I left for Louisiana where I would conduct the memorial service for a cousin who had died. I returned home Monday night from the funeral and went straight to Van's room. He was sitting up and looking very alert. We talked about the trip I had made, the memorial service, some of our relatives, and other issues. He then shocked me with the statement: "Dad, I think I am going to die soon, or God is healing me." I inquired why he felt that way. He replied, "It is said that when a person who has been sick for some time is about to die, he often has a few days of very good health and is able to think very clearly. It's like a gift from God to get one's house in order before leaving this world. I have felt so good the past few days, I think the Lord is healing me or my death is near." I responded, "Son, let's pray a miracle is occurring and you're being healed." That night, it was hard for me to sleep. I was restless; that eerie discussion with Van returned periodically throughout the night and into the next day. I later realized that Van had embraced his future, whatever it might be. There was no morbid or gleeful attitude as he talked with me, but it was very peaceful in terms of what he said and how he said it.

The following day, Tuesday, February 26, around 1:00 P.M. in the afternoon, Van awakened from a nap and was listless. He didn't feel like sitting with us in the kitchen-TV area as long as usual. He had no appetite and ate nothing. Within forty-eight hours, he went to be with the Lord. However, instead of being in excruciating pain and losing control of his body in any of the ways he had dreaded, Van died very peacefully without pain. Thanks be to the Lord!

AT HOME

The third reason we say Van had a good death is because he died at home. All of us feared he might have to be hospitalized or placed in hospice care the last weeks or months of his illness.

Van was also concerned that he was a burden to his mother and me. During the closing weeks of his life, he was very weak. It was difficult for him to get in and out of the shower, though he managed to do so right up until the time of his death. (An act of mercy was extended to us from some wonderful friends. Lilly Faye had mentioned that it was getting more difficult for Van to take a shower, so these generous friends sent a plumber to our house who rearranged things to make bathing easier.)

One day, about a month before his death, the home nurse told us that Van was worried about his mother and me. He had asked her to look into having him placed in a full-time care facility. Lilly Faye and I decided that we needed to come to an understanding with him that would serve all of us. We told him that when it was clearly better for him to be somewhere other than home, we would do all we could to place him in a good facility. However, until that time came, the three of us would work together to keep him at home. It was important for us to provide the daily care for him as long as we could. God had placed a deep desire in us to be very hands-on with Van; we wanted to be there for him until the very end. For him to die at home was a great victory for all of us.

THE GOODNESS OF GOD

At this juncture, let me go back to my purposes in sharing these intimate details about how Van died. It is to thank the Lord that, by all accounts, Van's death was a good one. Each time I think afresh about the circumstances surrounding his leaving, I am moved to say, "Thank you," to our Heavenly Father once again.

Also, it is to say to my family and friends who mourn his leaving that the goodness of God will continue to support us in the future just as He sustained Van in the closing hours of his life. His promise to never forsake us in the time of our need is real! We can predict future activity of God by looking at how He has sustained us in the past.

Lilly Faye and I do not want to inadvertently give the impression that anyone who died with different circumstances is not loved or blessed by God. I know there are good people who lose loved ones in the military, in plane crashes, and in other ways that are very emotionally painful. I would not judge these people, their deaths, or their families as being any less important to them as was Van to us. This is a testimony of one man and one family. It is not meant to be held up as the model of the only way a family can rejoice in the death of a loved one.

WITH FAMILY AND FRIENDS

The fourth good thing about Van's death was that family and best friends surrounded him right up to his last breath. In the last weeks of his life, Lilly Faye or I was always with him. Thankfully, there were times someone would come to stay with him while we went shopping or out to eat; there were literally countless offers to help out in this way. However, on that last Tuesday and Wednesday we were at his side around the clock. Rose and Carla came to the house on Tuesday and never left him except for brief periods. He was alert and able to talk with us at length. He also spoke with each of his nephews by phone. We all had a chance to tell him again how much we loved him, and he was able to acknowledge our expressions of love. One of the most precious memories I have is seeing Rose and Carla in bed with him—one on either side with him in the middle. What a tender moment that was! I felt in that instant I saw all three of them as small children again. I've relived that scene a dozen times since Van died!

There were many good friends who came to stay with us that last day and into the early morning hours when he died. Some brought food. Some six or seven friends gathered around Van's bed and sang "Amazing Grace." When Van died just after midnight, many of these wonderful people were still with us, and some even stayed for the next few hours until the authorities came to pick up his body.

There were so many people who highly esteemed Van. Hundreds of people at the First Baptist Church in Katy loved and admired him. One person referred him to as "The Pied Piper of Katy." A deacon and his wife told us recently that the church had adopted Van as their own; it was as though he belonged to the entire church. He and I preached dialogue sermons on Father's Day (See Section II for transcripts of the sermons). We also sang together on Father's Day and at Christmas during the intermission of the church pageant. One

Sunday school department requested he and I do an entire concert together, which failing health on his part never allowed us to do.

The people of the city of Katy also loved Van. He received calls, e-mail messages, gifts of money, and other expressions of love. Sunday School classes at the First United Methodist Church sent him a "love offering" on more than one occasion. He spoke at several churches in the area, and about five hundred copies of his recorded testimony have been requested.

Katy Mayor Hank Schmidt asked Van to walk the first lap with him at a citywide American Cancer Society walkathon. The next year, the planning committee for this annual event invited Van to be the keynote speaker. Many citizens of Katy were interested in Van's health status and calls came almost daily to check on him. The month after Van died, the annual walkathon to raise funds for the Cancer Society was held again in Katy. This time, around thirty of his friends dubbed themselves "Van's Fans" and walked the marathon in his memory.

We knew when Van died that there were many people who were standing with him and us, even if they were not physically in our house. The joy of knowing this is hard to put into words. His was not a lonely death; his was not a pitiful passing away. There were more people connected to us than we could number. I heard the story of a man whose son died in an accident in Europe while traveling. The father said one of the hardest things for him was not being with his son when the boy died—not having family and friends around. To think that his son had died so far from home was hard for him to get out of his mind. I shudder to think of how much harder it would have been for our family if Van had died while he was in Spain, or away from God and from family! I praise God for the strong support from family and friends.

LOVING RELATIVES

Related to that idea is yet another reason we think Van died in the midst of wonderful circumstances: his relatives loved and rallied around him in a very supportive way. The Sunday evening he gave his testimony at church, around thirty of them were present. When we gave an invitation at the end of the service for people to respond to what God was saying to them, around a hundred people flooded to the front of the auditorium. One was a nephew of ours who said he came forward simply to stand by Van to show his love and respect for his cousin.

Relatives were so kind to us. They sent cards and food, and helped in many ways. They visited Van in the hospital and later came to our house to see him. They prayed with him, read him scriptures, and wept with him. They told him how much they admired him and the ways God was using his testimony to bless the lives of others.

A STRONG, POSITIVE PERSONALITY

A sixth reason for our rejoicing in the way that Van died relates to his wonderful personality throughout his final days. He has always been known for his sharp personality and ability to entertain. He was quick on his feet and could keep everyone laughing for hours. We are so thankful that he never lost that great sense of humor. He was a truly funny guy, right up to the end.

On one occasion, Van and one of his aunts began writing each other the most outrageous things they could imagine: "I am in Istanbul, working for the CIA and looking for a well-known terrorist. I had to fight off a gang of thugs and barely escaped with my life by jumping off a steep cliff to the waters below where I swam out to a boat waiting for me." It was silly, funny, and typical of Van (and my sister).

On the day Van died, about ten hours before he actually passed on, our family was in his bedroom. One of us began to cry, and before long we were all crying. Van opened his eyes, looked around at us, and said, "You people look pitiful; I'm not dead yet!" The day before he had said to a good friend, in a joking manner, "I've not yet seen the light," referring to the tunnel and light some people see in near-death experiences.

I mentioned earlier that Van had gone with Rose to look at a house she and Mark were interested in buying. He got out of the car and Rose pulled his oxygen bottle as he walked slowly behind her, holding on to her shoulder. When they walked into the house, the realtor met them at the door and, according to Rose, was shocked to see this tall, thin, obviously very sick young man. She was without words, just looking at them. Van spoke up and said, "These brain tumors are terrible on one's health and looks, aren't they?"

About two weeks before Van died, a bit hyper from steroids and sleeping during the day, he stayed up very late one night and called several of his friends and relatives, not realizing how late it was. The sister I mentioned earlier said she was awakened by his call and they spent a long time talking about earlier experiences. When he realized how late it was, he was embarrassed. We all laughed about this for the next couple of days.

Van lost his edge on humor the last four or five hours of his life, but he never became sour or bitter in any way. What a gift from God: to have our son slip out of this world and into the presence of God with his personality intact! "Thank you, dear Lord."

A BITTERSWEET FAREWELL

The seventh reason we find joy in the events surrounding Van's death is because of the wonderful and uplifting atmosphere during the memorial service. Van talked with his mother and me on several occasions about what he wanted to convey in the service. I found it both sad and interesting that he had a notebook with several pages of information about his funeral with suggestions of people who would participate, songs to be used, and scriptures to be read. He was specific that I should present the sermon. ("A short one," he had joked.)

Van wanted his family to be in charge. He wanted his sisters and nephews to have a key role. He asked his friends to give testimonies and requested certain music by the First Baptist Church choir.

The day started with extended family members and very close friends participating in the burial service. Our plan was to have the commitment service of the body at the graveside with only this group in attendance. Then we would have the memorial service at the church later that afternoon. Because the weather was brutally cold, it was suggested by funeral director Hank Schmidt that we gather at the chapel in the Funeral Home where the body was. After a song by Pat Robinson, Carla's mother-in-law, I asked people to give brief testimonies about Van. The tears and laughter began to flow freely as inspirational or funny stories were told. A couple of examples:

Ten-year old nephew Caleb wept as he told of how much he loved Van. He said that Van always had time for him and when in Dallas, would always go to his school to have lunch with him. He also said Van listened to him.

Peggy Green, a close friend from Kansas City, Kansas, told how she and Van had gone to see the movie "Titanic" together. She had originally protested, because she did not know how to swim and thought the movie might be too scary. However, she said, Van had reassured her that he was a certified lifeguard (he was) and he would be there for her. The night of the movie, they were to meet at the theater. A large crowd was milling around, waiting to get tickets for the show. She was looking for Van when she heard someone yelling her name, "Peggy! Peggy!" She looked in the direction of the voice and saw the crowd opening up and someone walking in her direction. To her shock, it was Van! He had an inner tube around his waist, goggles on his face, flippers on his feet, and a snorkel on his head. He also had a water pistol, which he squirted into the audience from time to time—"For realism," he said.

Jennifer Philpot of New York City related how, as small children living in Mexico with their missionary parents, she and Van had talked about marrying each other when they became adults. She told of how he was a big brother to her when she entered Baylor University and how much she enjoyed coming to our home in San Antonio. She told us she had been in contact with Van during the recent months and was reminded how much he would encourage her even though he was desperately ill. He would say to her, "Jennifer, this is something you can do. You have so much in your favor, there is no way you and God, working together, can fail."

Brad Beasley, a roommate from days at Baylor University, said that when he thought of Van, he always thought about how unbelievably funny he was. He told of occasions when someone would come to visit at the house they rented. Van would start out by saying, "Would you like something cold to drink? Or perhaps you'd like some hot tea. Would you like some Brie and crackers? May we offer you a meal?" Brad would think, "What is he talking about? We don't have any of those things." They hardly ever had anything in the house to eat or drink as they had very little money among the three of them.

We also laughed when it was mentioned that Van used his gas card to take his dates to the station near the Baylor campus for refreshments. Since he had no money most of the time, with the card he could at least buy gas, ride around town, and finish the date with a coke and chips he and the girl bought at the gas station!

After lunch with family at the church, the memorial service began at two o'clock. The worship center was packed and people were standing in the foyer, unable to find a seat.

During the service, the combination of prayers, testimonies, music, a pictorial presentation of Van's life (including a video of his testimony given to the church) was mightily used of God. Everyone present was touched! On several occasions, people broke into applause. Three or four times the entire congregation spontaneously stood in worship and gratitude to God for His presence. One such time was when President Doug Hodo of Houston Baptist University presented us with a Master of Arts in Psychology Degree for Van.

A neighbor told me two days later that in all her years of attending memorial services, including having served as pianist in the church for decades, she had never participated in one more inspirational than Van's. Many others have since said the same to us. A pastor of one of the area's largest churches requested a video of the service and of Van's testimony to show to his congregation.

We also received many letters. The comments reflected on the high inspirational nature of the memorial service. Two examples are:

"Dear Charles: Please tell Lilly Faye that of all the funeral and memorial services that I have been to (including those I have done), Van's was the most glorifying to the Lord and honoring of the loved ones that I have ever witnessed. The truth was spoken in love in so many ways. How wonderful it is that we have a God who gives us all "do-overs."

Rev. Larry Smith, Th.D

"Dear Dr. and Mrs. Wisdom:

I have never been to a memorial service that was more moving or Christ-centered. Having never met Van, I left feeling personally touched by his life. In my opinion, no more meaningful praise could have been showered on a human being than the kinds of things that were said about your son. I came in hopes of being some encouragement to you, but left feeling like you had ministered to me in a profound way."
Rev. Del Fehsenheld, III
Life Action Ministries

One thing I emphasized at the memorial service and need to repeat is that the funeral was not about Van, but about God! Without Him, there would not be the wonderful stories of redemption and changed lives. I reminded all of us that any good thing we could possibly say about Van is because of the grace, mercy, love, forgiveness, and restoration of our great God as expressed in Jesus Christ. Therefore, this "good death" account is to His glory and no one else.

As Van had done some years earlier, we concluded the service by singing "Because He Lives, I can Face Tomorrow."

"In my beginning is my end.
In my end is my beginning."
T.S. Elliot[12]

"Our days are like grass;
We flourish like flowers of the field,
The wind passes over and we are gone,
and our place knows us no more.
But the steadfast love of the Lord abides forever."
Psalm 103

"I depart in peace for my eyes have seen your salvation.
You have shown me the path of life.
In your presence there is fullness of joy,
In Your right hand are pleasures forevermore."
Psalm 16
Comments Received After Van's Death

".... What a joyful heart! His testimony and his bravery inspire me greatly." D.H.

".... Van was pure sunshine in my life and I will always remember his love and craziness!" G.R.

".... Our family had gone through a difficult time this year and God used Van to get us successfully through it." A Father

".... I too have a 'can of worms' that needs to be opened; Van gave me the courage to start looking in that direction." J.D.

".... I played it (Van's testimony on tape) for my teenage grandchildren and others. They were moved to tears." R.R.B.

".... One of the messages that Van was able to convey so well is God's faithfulness to forgive and restore." J.A.

".... He always stopped to say 'hello' and give me a big hug at church, which meant so much to me." J.K.

".... From Van we learned to smile and keep faith no matter how terrible the adversity. No matter how sick he was he always lifted the spirits of those around him." Van's doctor

".... I am so thankful the Lord led me to Van. The anxiety and depression were unbearable when I first started seeing Van. His voice calmed my spirit. His wisdom is priceless. The skills necessary to cope he taught me have brought healing to my family and me." P.Y.

"…. The Lord sent the Holy Spirit to me through Van Wisdom, and I thank God every day for Van's compassion and his honesty. On March 2, 2000, I asked Jesus to come into my life. Had God not sent Van to me when He did, I might still be wandering around, a lost soul." L.D.P.

PART II

LESSONS MY SON TAUGHT ME

CHAPTER 5—"LIFE IS NOT A DRESS REHEARSAL"

On Sunday night, April 5, 1998, Van shared the following words with 800 people at the First Baptist Church in Katy, Texas. His purpose was to acknowledge the time in his life when he was away from God and the results of that very difficult time. Most of all, his message was about how the Lord had used circumstances to bring him back to the faith of his childhood. His words impressed upon the audience the importance of decisions and he urged us to remember, "Life is not a dress rehearsal!"

I'm here tonight to share with you concerning some of the experiences I've had in life. We've all heard that God created us and loves us. But we often rebel in life and want to "do our own thing." We can say to Him, *"I know you created us and want the best for us, but I think I can handle my life better than you."* I had that attitude.

This is a good, exciting story. I know that some of my choices have not been good, but as that song says, He's always there and He always loves you; you can come back any time.[1] That is what is exciting.

I've often thought, "What do people do who are struggling and do not know God? What do they do? To whom do they turn for help? A therapist? Maybe that will help them for a while. Do they go to close friends, maybe family members? What do they do if they have no belief system, if they don't have God to turn to?" I don't know what I would have done.

(*Pause*)

You'll have to excuse me . . . I am very nervous and may get choked up at times. Bear with me.

I'm so glad my parents minister in a church where I can come and share this with you. This I am about to tell you is not me, not my style. What I am going to tell you tonight is known only by about eight people in the world. This is not something I typically share about myself. But I'm grateful we're in a church where, when God asks me to come, I can do it. I would rather not be here, but God has told me to come and I have to be obedient to Him.

What I'm going to tell you is probably going to disappoint you. (*Pause. Emotional with voice trembling and tears in his eyes*) I've let you down, and I apologize for that. How you respond to what I say is between you and God.

I want to thank my family for being here tonight, loving and supporting me always. You know, when you live in a pastor's home—I'm the pastor's son, if you haven't made that connection yet. Charles Wisdom, Van Wisdom...we sort of share a name. (*Laughter*)

When you live in a pastor's home, there is a built-in insulation so that you don't share with people. There is the expectation in the church that you are supposed to be perfect and therefore we don't really share with each other. But God has brought our family to the place where we want to follow Christ and share our story with the world. We've held many things in for a long time and unfortunately that is the nature of the ministry. But now we want to deal with them as God tells us.

There's a song known by many of you, "Amazing Grace." When you have a reconnection with Christ, you really get to know His grace. My mom is reading a book right now by Philip Yancey <u>What's So Amazing About Grace?</u> In it, he says grace is defined as "nothing we can do that will make God love us more, and nothing we can do to make God love us less."[2] I want to repeat this because I'm not sure we always get it, or at least I don't always get it: "Grace is defined as nothing we can do to make God love us more and nothing we can do to make God love us less." The truth is, we're all conditional in our relationships and we always expect something back. But God offers grace; whatever we do, He is not going to love us any more nor love us any less. I'm experiencing grace; it's great. It's incredible to know that, in spite of some of the things I've done, He still loves me.

Some of the things I'm going to share with you, I'd rather you not know about me. There are other things I'd rather you know about me. I could make a list of things about me I'd rather you know about me, but that is not what God is telling me to do tonight.

As I said, growing up in a pastor's home, we had many good experiences. We were missionaries at one time in Mexico. There, I was molested as a young child and chose to not tell my parents about that experience. Unfortunately, there were other experiences with sexual molestation. This is not to make excuses about the way I approached life or the choices I later made. But it had an impact! Those experiences factored in as to the reason I made some choices.

In the second grade, a great thing happened to me: I became a Christian. It was while we were in Chicago and Dad was working on his Doctor of Ministry Degree. He was also interim pastor of the First Baptist Church of Dolton, and it was during that time I decided to become a follower of Christ. That was a very good decision and, in later years, I would see just how important it was. That relationship, that connection with Christ, paid off. Once you become a child of God, there are built in assurances that you may not (then) be aware of. I certainly was not fully aware as a second-grader. But as an adult, I have been able to look back and see how that one experience changed my life. (*Weeping*)

This testimony tonight might be the second most important experience in my life. So, I must be obedient and share with my church family.

Because of the sexual abuse, in spite of growing up in a Christian home, I had lots of doubts about my sexuality. "What kind of man am I? What kind of person do I want to be?" (Just let me say to young people or anyone who has experienced sexual abuse, if you haven't shared it with anyone yet, find someone safe in the youth department of the church to whom you can tell your story. Talk to a

A Voice From Heaven

Sunday School teacher. Tell your parents. That is one of the purposes of the church—to give assistance to those who are in need.)

As I was going through high school, playing on the tennis team, involved in many school activities, a member of the swim team, I was dating and having what I thought was a pretty good, normal life. My senior year I went to eight different proms around the city. In fact, my folks bought me a tux; it was cheaper owning my personal tuxedo rather than having to rent one each time I needed it. I was awarded a lot of opportunities, *even though no one knew what was going on inside of me.* (*Pause. Emotional*) I didn't tell any of my friends, I didn't tell my parents, I didn't tell my youth leaders. I didn't share this with anyone because I was so ashamed of the things that had happened in my life and the unconscious choices I was making. (*Emotional*) But I loved the church!! I loved being active in church, going to youth choir, camps in the summer, and many other activities. I thought to myself, "These are just struggles I'm having right now. When I get older, I'll get married, have kids, and all of this is going to work out at some point." But I wasn't making an effort to strengthen my relationship with Christ. I was attending church, but I was not building my relationship with Him.

In Second Corinthians, Paul is talking about a struggle he is having. We're not sure what it is, but he prayed that "the thorn in his flesh" would be removed.[3] I can remember going to youth camps and conferences and always going forward at altar call, just crying and crying, knowing that I had these struggles and self-doubts, but not knowing what to do. I didn't want to tell anyone about them. I decided that this was just a personal thing I would have to face.

So I went off to college and began having a great time. I made many new friends and became involved in many campus activities. In my senior year, I became involved with a group of friends and began to feel that maybe I was gay; maybe I was homosexual. I began to think that the reasons I had experienced these terrible things was because that was what I was "supposed" to be; maybe God had created me to be homosexual. I don't have the answers why that was my struggle. I began to think that it did not matter *why* I am who I am, but that was just the way things were going to be. I had lots of self-doubt. And the *freedom* I found in doing what I wanted to do, while on one hand liberating, <u>it was a miserable freedom</u>! It was not a freedom about "I finally feel good about who I am," but a miserable freedom, "I'm going to do things my own way and if people don't like it, that is their problem!"

After I graduated from college, I had a chance to go live and work in Spain. There, no one knew me; they didn't know I was a pastor's kid or anything else about me. I could create a whole new life for myself. I did that. There, I found people who would encourage whatever choices I made. Unfortunately, I made some very bad choices. Instead of moving toward Christ, my choices led me further and further away from Him.

Yet, always in the back of my mind, whenever I was at some function or involved in some of these activities, I just never felt right. "Oh sure, let's go do this, or whatever," I'd say to my friends. But you know, have you ever been right in the middle of something and you would be saying to yourself, "This just doesn't feel right; this is wrong"? I don't know if any of you have ever experienced that: just continue doing something that didn't seem right, but you kept on doing it. I have experienced that; I've lived it. You persist in pursuing something because you say to yourself, "This other way is just too hard!" You start doubting whether Christ will accept you. "Will He want me in spite of these things I've done?"

The time came for me to make a decision about staying in Spain or coming back to the States. I wanted to be close to my family and have a relationship with them. So I decided to come home, yet not letting them know of my struggle. I kept those things to myself. I continued to think, "I'm going to be okay. I'll get married and have a family and all this is going to work out one day. I'm really going to do it! One day I'm going to get my act together.

I came back to Houston and I really believe God placed me in a position He wanted me to have. I went to work in Social Services and, of all places, I wound up working with sexually abused kids. During that time, I began to clue in that, maybe what had happened to me, being sexually abused, was the reason for the problems I had. But then, I didn't want to think that way. I would say to myself, "That really isn't me!" I kind of had two memories of myself and intentionally connected with the one I liked. After all, that is the way we think, isn't it? We like to see ourselves in a positive light.

The next job I had (in Social Services) was working with terminally ill persons. I learned a lot from those people and that they really wanted to live life. One of the things I said to my patients was, "You know, life is not a dress rehearsal. We've got one chance and we've got to make it work." But as I was telling them that, I was saying to myself, "Van, your life is not a dress rehearsal either. You've got to get things right in your own life!" All during this time, I was continuing to meet people and, from the world's standards, I was having a good time. Outwardly I was okay, but inwardly I was miserable!! It wasn't where I wanted to be. I worked with a Mexican lady and we always spoke Spanish to each other. She would say, "Van, *eres hijo de Dios*; you are a child of God and He is not going to let you be comfortable until you are doing what He wants you to do!" And it is so true: God does not care about our comfort; He cares about our character. A lot of us think He is concerned about how comfortable we are on earth—not so! He is more concerned about what kind of character we develop.

Shortly thereafter, working with these people who had terminal illnesses, I learned that I tested positive for the HIV virus. (*Emotional. Long pause*) You know, it's like you get blasted with a slap in the face: **Boom!!** You know, I'm twenty-whatever years old and now all the hopes and dreams I once had, I might not get to pursue. (*Crying*) It's because of very, very bad choices I had made. Now when that happened, you'd think I would say to myself, "Boy, I've got to get my act together. I've got to get active in church and do things right. Who knows how much time I may have left!" (*Pause*) I did just the opposite! Whereas before I had not really accepted all my struggles and would feel guilty, now I just "gave in" and fully entered that lifestyle. The devil was telling me, "Well man, you really don't have a chance now. You'll never get it all together now. You'll definitely never get married now and have children; who would want you? You probably won't live very long. Now, some of your graduate dreams are gone! Who is going to want you but *that* community? They deal with HIV and AIDS all the time; they'll be the only ones who will love and accept you." But it is interesting that since that diagnosis,

I haven't heard from any of those "friends." Nevertheless, the devil was telling me I was stuck in my lifestyle and that there was no need of turning back. "Just get with those people who will accept you." Of course, I was still miserable but I was trying to convince myself otherwise.

As I look back now, I know that God had placed me in those positions of working with kids who had been sexually abused, with cancer and AIDS patients. He did that because I came to learn that I needed to be ministered to; it wasn't about helping those other people but getting help for myself! And God had orchestrated all of this.

(*Pause. Emotional*) Of course there came a time when I had to tell my parents. (*Pause. Weeping*) And I'm so sorry! I have great parents; they're cool people. I like being around them, which makes it even harder when you disappoint them. Not only do they minister, they live it! This is the way they live at home. They're not kidding; they believe this and they are passionate about it. They're not just here on Sundays and then they go home and do their own thing and he collects a paycheck. This is not how they live their lives. They truly live their lives passionately for Christ.

One of my concerns when I learned that I had tested positively for HIV, "If anyone learns about this, my dad has lost his job!" The ministry they had been called into might be jeopardized by my bad choices. That was overwhelming for me to think about. Of course I came home and told them and we prayed and they cried. They told me "We love you and we are here for you." It was the response Christ would have. We had some struggles because, at that point, I still wanted to do my own thing. I just wanted their love. But one verse my mom had quoted to me whenever I allowed them to talk to me about this subject was Philippians 1:6 which says, "Being confident that He who began a good work in you will carry it on unto completion, until the day of Jesus Christ." She was saying, "He who began a good work in you, God, He started a good work in you in second grade when you decided to follow Him. He's not going to give up on you. You're not going to be comfortable until His work is complete in you and that means returning to what you know is His plan!"

A Voice From Heaven

I'm sure some of you are thinking, "This boy grew up, active in church. How did all this happen to him? How did he get to this point? He had role models in and out of the church. He wanted to love Christ, wanted to serve Christ, wanted to grow up and become a deacon. How did all of this happen to him?" I don't know. I don't have the answers for those questions. Bad choices, bad experiences as a child, I suppose, are a major part of the answer. But I am now confident that He is saying to me, "No matter what you've done, you can still come home. I'm here for you. You can come back. At one point you made a decision to follow me; now come on back because I'm here for you." I was also encouraged because my parents were always telling me, "We love you; we're here for you; we will support you. We're praying for you." (*Weeping*) One of the things my dad said to me that made me feel so good was, " Van, if you ever get sick, it would be an honor for me to take care of you. If you are ever too sick to take care of yourself, I want to take care of you." One of the first things I had thought about when I learned I was HIV positive was, "It would not be right for me to ask them to help me in any way; I brought this upon myself." But here he was, saying, "I want to take care of you." I never asked them; he volunteered that offer. I thought to myself, "Isn't that just what Christ would do?" Dad offered that help.

Last summer I was in a job I loved. I was semi-miserable in many ways, but telling myself I was doing fine. I had a good career. I had moved home for a couple of months so I could save money to buy a house. I thought; "I'm doing well with my HIV; I haven't had any problems." Then, my company was bought out and two weeks later I was diagnosed with Hodgkin's Disease (which was, by the way, not related to my HIV). Then, all the top people at work were fired and I lost my job. Within two weeks, I was sitting in a chemo-chair, losing my hair, and thinking to myself, "How did all this happen in a month?" Up to that time, I was healthy, exercising, making plans for a great future. Now, I have no job, no opportunities, (*laughing*) and no hair. Now, I tell you that in all these happenings, God gave me "a gift." It was the first time my family could say in a public forum, "Pray for Van; he needs your prayers!" The church has responded **wonderfully**. For the past months, I have been receiving, each week, phone calls, letters, and cards: all letting me know I was the object of your prayers. I have seen what I experienced as a child; you guys have been walking billboards of God's love! That is one of the reasons I'm telling my story tonight. As I said, I really don't want to do this. I know now that I run the risk that every time one of you sees me in the church, "That's the pastor's son, the guy who struggled with being gay." I know some of you won't think that, but many of you might. If that's your response, I understand, and it is between you and God.

So, last summer as I went through these losses, it got down pretty much to just God and me! There was not a whole lot left that could be taken away. It wasn't that I was fearful of dying; my fear became, *(weeping) "I'm never going to experience in this life the great, abundant life God wants me to have!!"* It was all because I had wanted to do things my way! That's it. It wasn't God saying, "You know, you'd better get your life together or some real bad things are going to happen." Rather God was saying to me in all of that, "Van, I really do love you and I want to have a relationship with you. I want you to go to bed at night in peace. Every time you get a cold, I don't want you to feel guilty about getting sick because of your past; I want you to have peace." It dawned upon me: that's what He really wants for me. He wants me to have peace and be happy. I've been chasing this other way and He's been standing here all the time saying, "Just turn around; I'm here waiting for you! I love you!"

One thing I was thinking about when I was preparing this testimony for you comes from my days of playing tennis. When you'd start warming up for a game, if you were playing with someone you knew well, and you'd serve a bad serve, you could say, "Hey, you know I wasn't quite ready. Let me do that over; give me a 'do-over.'" Or you might say to your friend, "I could tell you were not ready; go ahead and start again; take a 'do-over.'" My dad is a golfer and in golf it's known as a "mulligan;" you get to take an extra swing. Well, you know, that's what God offers all of us. *(Weeping)* Anytime in our lives when we fail Him, He says, "Why don't you take a 'do-over'? I don't care where you've been, I don't care what you've done, I care about **you**. You can take a 'do-over'!" I say, "You know God, I wasn't focused; I wasn't ready. That's not what I wanted." God says, "You can take a 'do-over'. And you can do that anytime!"

Since that time, since I've taken a 'do-over' and recommitted my life to Him, *it's so nice to go to bed at night!* To feel His peace, His grace. Those songs and stories you hear at church make sense. They made sense a long time ago and somehow I lost that. *(Weeping)*

Sadly enough, with my 'do-over,' as with all our 'do-overs,' there are consequences in life. My situation, the one I'm very aware of, is my health status. I need to monitor my health. "Am I getting a cold? What is the next health problem I may have to face? Why can I not run a mile as fast as I once did? Why can't I do the things I once was able to do with ease?" There was a time in my life when I challenged myself with strong goals. Now I am concerned about making sure I can get up in the morning and I schedule my life around chemo appointments. It's the consequences of making bad choices in my life.

Gratefully, with the 'do-over,' I have someone to go to now, don't I? Whereas before I had all these people around me saying, "Oh, you're okay. Do whatever your heart tells you to do. You're a good person." (I do have to tell you that I needed those people in those times.) But there are serious consequences to the bad choices I have made. I don't know what the future holds for me or what opportunities I may have. Five years ago I planned my life on a seventy- to eighty-year scale; now I have to do a six-months deal. That's the reality of my life, you know. I had talked to one of our members about applying to law school one time, but I don't know if those are realities for me. Maybe they are and I'm sure God is going to give me a peace about what my future holds. I do know it is time for me to stop doing what I want to do and start doing what God wants me to do!!

My dad and I met with a gentleman this week about starting a ministry with a Baptist association for people who, either they or family members, struggle with homosexuality or sexual abuse. If they can't come to the church and say, "Hey, I'm having a tough time in this way in my life"—if they don't come to the churches, they will go other places. I've been to those other places. Those people tell you some nice things in the beginning, but it's not that great at the end. It's like I said earlier, I haven't heard from any of my former friends since they learned I am HIV positive.

I want to thank all of you for coming tonight and loving me regardless. That song earlier, "God Doesn't Care Where You're Coming From," was great. I think the actual title is, "Jesus Doesn't Care," and when I saw it in the bulletin, I thought to myself, "This must be a typo!" *(Congregational laughter)* I'm so thankful I have a church that loves me and that my dad's job is not in jeopardy. Those are real concerns I had. I had thought, "If these people ever know about me, what are they going to think? Are they still going to love me? Will they still walk up and hug me? Will they be fearful when I am talking with their child?" When I arrived at church tonight, I saw some of you in the parking lot and I thought to myself, "I love these people. I don't want them to know these things about me. Maybe I'll just walk away and we can have a guest speaker—another guest speaker." *(Congregational laughter)* But that's not what God wanted me to do.

If any of you want to talk, have concerns or have family members, friends, and you want someone to talk to, I'm available.

It's nice to come home. *(Weeping)* I'm grateful for a God who shows His love by saying, "You can come home anytime you want." On top of that, I have a church that says, "Come home whenever you want." And a choir, family members, relatives, aunts and uncles, all saying, "We love you; we don't care. You can come home whenever you want."

A song that meant much to me as a child, I think of a lot now. I'm not really worried about my future; I've got Christ, don't I? This song stands out in my mind. I'm going to sing the chorus of it now. Don't listen to the quality of the voice as much as listen to the words. They mean a lot.

(Without musical accompaniment)

"Because He lives, I can face tomorrow.
Because He lives, all fear is gone.
Because I know, I know He holds the future.
And life is worth the living, just because He lives."

Thank You.

At the end of his testimony, the congregation stood and applauded for five minutes without stopping. People began to move in great numbers to the front of the auditorium where Van was standing by his mother. They began to embrace him, weeping with him, assuring him of their love. Several told of friends or family members who struggled with some of the same issues he had. Many asked to spend time with him over lunch or in a counseling session. The overwhelming response of the people that night, plus over 500 others who requested a copy of his testimony, led to the start of a ministry known as NEW BEGINNINGS in the church. Van also became part of the church staff as counselor for three years before he died.

In addition to the face-to-face encounters with people after that night, Van received many letters that sincerely thanked him for his honesty and humility.

Van,

There have been occasions in my life when I felt compelled to write from my heart. Tonight, after hearing your testimony, I knew it was once again time to do so.

This evening my father, Bobby, Janet, and I went to the service together and as soon as we got into the car after church, Bobby said, "That is the most courageous thing I've ever seen in my life." Bobby took the words out of my mouth, because that is exactly what I was thinking and feeling in my heart.

The words that kept going through my mind during your testimony were honor, courage, bravery, and repentance. This applies not only to you, but also to your whole family. I am honored to belong to a church and I feel fortunate to be ministered to by a man such as your father.

I believe that most people go throughout life hiding behind masks and false identities, while frequently feeling guilt and shame for things that they have done and cannot take back. We have all done things in our lives that we are ashamed of or feel guilty about doing, however, that which differentiates us is not only our repentance, but also the actions we take once we have accepted these poor decisions and actions.

There are very few people in this world that would have the courage to testify what you did tonight and you should be proud of yourself; not for this fact alone, but for who you are. I believe your testimony will give others strength to make decisions that will have positive impact in their own lives.

Thank you for sharing your testimony with me this evening; you not only gave a wonderful message, but you delivered it so sincerely with true humility, and that makes you the greatest warrior that could ever exist. As I told you after the service, I could use a friend like you.

I pray that when you look at yourself in the mirror, that you do love yourself and are proud of what you see. I am truly happy for you, because you are embarking on a brand new life. When I see you in church or anywhere else, I will point at you and say, "That is a man to be honored."

With love and respect,
JS

CHAPTER 6—LESSONS VAN TAUGHT ME

I have indicated elsewhere in this book that Van and I sometimes exchanged positions as teacher-learner. In the last few years of his life, I was amazed at how much God was teaching me through Van's life and insights. A few of these teachings are as follow.

1. Van taught me not to jump to conclusions about what is in a person or what he is truly committed to. There may be the potential for a very deep love for God and the things of heaven in one who, at other times, seems to be "non-spiritual."
Until Van came to the place of giving his testimony and returning in his heart to the Lord, I felt he was not truly interested in spiritual matters. I feared he was so locked into himself that he just didn't have time for the Lord. I was wrong!! The remaining four or five years of his life revealed just the opposite. His deep interests in the things of God were covered by the messiness of his life and the influence of those around him.
Each time Van was in the hospital, it was inspirational for us to see how often he got around to sharing his faith with those who worked there, regardless of whether they were housecleaning personnel, nurses, or doctors. On one occasion, he asked his oncologist's permission to pray for him. Another time, while in intensive care, a male nurse found it easy to share with Van that he was having marital difficulties. When Van was transferred to a regular hospital

room, that nurse returned on three occasions for counseling. And then there was a young African-American man who was delighted when he learned that Van's dad was a Baptist pastor since his dad also was pastor of a church. He and Van prayed together.

I have always felt God had given me some insight into human behavior. One can imagine, therefore, my amazement at how easy Van could reach in and draw out the essence of a particular situation. His insights were uncanny. I remarked to Lilly Faye that God seemed to have endowed him with supernatural understanding at the time of his return to the Lord.

The last eighteen months of his illness, even to the last week or so, I would come home each evening from the church and share with Van the activities of the day. Almost every evening, I would go to bed having gained some new insight about what had occurred that day. I came to treasure those times with him.

2. *Van taught me that very hard times have the potential to destroy you or they can make you much stronger.*
Van and I talked often about what he had to endure with his trauma of being sexually assaulted as a child, his HIV status, and the memory of his foolish choices. I watched him struggle with these realities. I read his diary where he expressed concern about bad decisions he had made. I heard him talk about the limited time he had on this earth. I told him on more than one occasion, "Son, what you are going through in your struggle with HIV will crush you or make you much stronger." There is no doubt of the outcome.

For instance, the topic of death would often surface. Hesitant to face that painful fear, either Lilly Faye or I would often say something like, "Van, you're doing so well. Who knows? There may be a discovery for HIV infected persons that will make it possible for you to live a normal length life." I never stopped praying for a miracle. In many instances, ministers or other devout Christians would come in groups to pray over him, often anointing him with oil. There were people throughout the world praying for Van's health. He, however, without being morbid about it, always sought to bring us back to reality. He did not want to nurse false hopes or give us reason to do so. He said his goal was to balance living as normal a life as he could while, at the same time, keeping the big picture in mind.

We felt living with the prospect of facing death made him tougher in many ways. Six weeks before his death, at a party honoring him hosted by members of the *New Beginnings* ministry, Van spoke to the group about keeping faith in the face of whatever they might encounter. He told them to keep their eyes fixed on the Lord and trust Him for the outcome of whatever they might face. There were many tears shed that evening. I was stunned by this simple display of inner strength. I thought of Paul's words to the Corinthians, "Even though our outward man perish, yet the inward man is renewed day by day."[1]

3. *Van taught me it is much better to "embrace your story" than it is to expend tons of energy covering it up.* To face up to one's life, "warts and all," and put the story out there in a transparent manner will have the following results:

a) This will honor the Lord and motivate Him to pour out great blessings on the persons involved. I, as well as family members and friends, are amazed at the richness of life the Lord gave Van once he faced his situation and took steps to do something about it. "A miracle," and "Only God could explain what is going on in Van's life and the way he is touching so many people," are statements we continue to hear even today.

b) The person who is transparently telling his story will be "set free" in ways never imagined! Heavy burdens will be lifted. There will be a sense of experiencing a new beginning in so many ways. There will be deep satisfaction with self and with life. No wonder the term "born again" is used in the scripture as one way of describing what is occurring.

c) It will encourage others to step forth and share their story, as well. After Van gave his testimony at the church, an amazing number of people came to him saying, "I have wanted to talk about this situation that has bothered me for years. Your honesty has helped me to be honest with myself."

4. *Van taught me to love people who struggle with same-sex attraction.* A homosexual, like any sinner, may be a very good person in the sense that he or she may be searching for God "in all the wrong places." Van, and participation in Exodus International, helped me to see those persons entangled in homosexuality as people Jesus loves dearly and for whom He died. Primarily through Van's influence, I lost my resentment of them and began to see them as they are: family members, neighbors, co-workers, or just acquaintances who harbor deep hurts in their lives.

At the four Exodus International conferences we have attended in the past ten years, Lilly Faye and I have marveled at the testimonies of hundreds of adults who have found freedom from their struggles with same-sex involvement. We learned that the majority of them had been sexually abused as children. Others are honest to say that they are in the midst of an internal battle, seeking peace but have not found it yet. The atmosphere among these dear people is one of dynamic encounter with God. They are desperate because this insidious lifestyle is so intensively wicked and eventually absorbs the very life out of them. They know that a half-hearted, lukewarm relationship with "religion" is not going to get the job done. Their zeal is powerful!

Van taught me to always seek balance between *compassion* and *conviction* in regard to those ensnared by homosexuality.

5. *Van taught me that I am as much a sinner and am as broken as any homosexual or other person whose choices in life set them apart as "obvious sinners."*
Walking with Van through his struggles and getting to know his story, as well as that of people associated with Exodus, became a mirror to me, to help me see my sinful heart and true brokenness. What I knew intellectually became an experienced reality. I must be very careful in pointing at the sins of others without first being able to see the potential for sin and evil that is in my own heart!

I have come to reassert in my heart that there is an on-going struggle to pull away from God: to take Him for granted and be satisfied with a half-hearted relationship with Him. More than ever,

I see in my life the need of periodic repentance. As the hymn says, "Prone to wander . . . prone to leave the God I love."[2]

6. *Van taught me the wholesomeness of laughter; that I needed to "lighten up" from time to time.*

Van loved life and loved to laugh. He loved to entertain others and make them laugh as well. He never had people laugh by pointing out someone else's shortcomings. He was a creative personality and able to say things or act in very funny ways. Even in his last days, as he was obviously growing weaker, he laughed and caused others to do the same. It was not a "gallows" laugh. It was sincere and from the heart.

7. *Van taught me to identify with the underdog.*

He exemplified the "protector's" profile. It was not a "rescue" or "co-dependent" position he took. It was a matter of being sensitive to people, picking up on their hurts and trying to help them in appropriate ways. God instructs us to lift the fallen, to identify with those in need and respond in the way that He would if He were on earth. <u>Be sensitive to over-weight people, poor people, minority people, fearful people, lost people, weak people.</u>

8. *Van taught me to keep length of life in proper perspective; that even those who live a long time on earth are here only a short time.*

An intellectual awareness has become very real to me. To see my son, a young, strong, vibrant man, slowly waste away reminds me that I am a fool if I live my life as though I'm going to live forever in this world. The only person Jesus ever called a *fool* during his earthly ministry was the man in Luke chapter 12 who planned his life as though he would live a long, long time.

9. *Van taught me that, next to my relationship with my Creator, nothing or no one is as important as my family members.*

To say that family counts is trite. I felt I always loved my family as much as anybody cared for their loved ones. But now, each child and grandchild is somehow more precious, more "valuable" to me. I cherish them more. Having lost Van in this life, I yearn to be connected with my grandchildren as much as possible.

10. *Van taught me that, except for the loss of a spouse, the death of a child is the hardest loss a person can experience.*

As a friend who lost an adult daughter told me, "The hole in your heart will never go away. With time, however, you'll not fall into it as much." I spoke to a gathering of men after Van died, and it was a tough thing to do. I mentioned the death of Van and how hard it had been on my wife and me. Afterwards, a well-meaning man came up to say that he was sorry to hear of Van's death. He said, "I know it's hard to lose a loved one; my father died a year ago and it has been tough on me every since." I agree it is very hard to lose a father. I have lost my father and mother, as well as my father-in-law and mother-in-law. My wife and I loved our parents very much and miss them greatly. But the death of Van has been tougher on Lilly Faye and me than the loss of all of them put together. Maybe that is not the testimony of others, but it is definitely true of us!

The death of Van would have been difficult at any time, of course, but the time of his passing gave me pause to wonder. After all, he had come back to the Lord, resulting in open doors of ministry and changed lives by the hundreds. I was certain God was going to give him a truly impacting ministry, maybe even on an international level as he had shared his story in Latin America, Europe, and the Middle East. He had more opportunities than he could accept to speak and counsel with individuals, couples, and families. After all, he was "Exhibit A" of God's mercy, love, forgiveness, and restoration. What a great future! "Surely God is going to heal Van," I thought.

He did, but not on this earth.

11. *Van taught me that I do not have to be afraid to die.*

When he first learned he was HIV positive, he was scared. All of us were scared. When he learned he had Hodgkin's disease, he knew the time he had left on this earth had been greatly shortened. Across the six years he fought this cancer, he became more and more unafraid. Part of it had to do with his renewed faith, and his resulting ministry to a growing number of people. But the secret is that he learned to live with the tension of, on one hand, having a life-threatening disease and, on the other hand, being optimistic about what life he had left. <u>I never heard Van complain, blame God, doctors, or anyone else</u>. He would say, "We can lick this" (whatever the latest problem was) and also say, "If my time is short, I just have to face it straight on." I saw him slowly and deliberately embrace his pending death. He did not give up until the last day when he slowly began to slip into semi-consciousness. Looking back, it is easy to see how he almost welcomed his death. When he said to me just two nights before he died, "I'm either going to die soon, or God is healing me," he was proclaiming his acceptance of whichever it might be!! Apart from some catastrophe, I am more secure in my innermost being that when it comes time for me to leave this earth, I will not be afraid nor fight it.

12. *Van taught me to "get radical" about my ministry.*

He did this indirectly by dying young and having limited time to serve the Lord on this earth. I'm sure it is partly from my age, but I feel that I, too, have a short time left to prepare others and myself for eternal life. I don't want to waste any time "playing church." If I make a mistake of being too zealous or too reserved in sharing the Gospel, I want to err on the side of being too aggressive.

A friend once gave me a Bible with the following inscription:

"Charlie, always remember:
' *'Tis only one life,*
'Twill soon be past.
Only what's done
For Christ will last.'"

CHAPTER 7 — VANISMS

It has been observed that life is like a collection of beautiful pearls, each one, individually, of great value. Then, when you string them together, they are even more valuable.

Each of Van's experiences, standing alone, is precious. Combining them into a seamless work of God, however, exponentially adds to the impact of what he taught in the closing years of his life.

In the four years of Van's ministry after his return to Jesus Christ, he gained a limited amount of fame as a result of his frequent use of short, pithy statements about life. Obviously, not all of them were original to him. Others were. The following is a list of some of those and the meaning they had for him:

"Accept God's Grace"
Van was overwhelmed by the grace of God. He spoke of it in his testimony and often called on Christians to both receive and offer grace. In Van's thinking, one of the greatest needs of the church is to be intentional about demonstrating grace. In public he was hesitant to be critical of the church. In private, he told me he had known many homosexuals who were desperate and would love to have a safe, grace-filled church to attend and sort things out in their hearts. However, they felt apathy or condemnation from most of the churches they visited. They chose to stay away and hurt in silence.

A statement that had greatly encouraged him is by Philip Yancey: "Grace means there is nothing you can do to make God love you more, and nothing you can do to make God love you less."[1] Since he had been the recipient of the Lord's grace, Van was continually focused on it. In his counseling and in his preaching, he came back to this subject time and again. His eagerness to offer grace to people who had turned their backs on the things of God was effective in helping him reach others.

Unconditional love is very hard for many of us. People who are vastly different from us in belief or behavior are more easily handled by just ignoring them. Sexual brokenness, in particular, is a major hindrance to many in the church. Van was an advocate for these people. He sought to echo the philosophy of Joe Dallas who had said in a sermon at First Baptist Church of Katy, "The Christian's response to homosexuals or any other person with sexual brokenness must be a balance between compassion and conviction. Historically, the church has had the *conviction* part down fairly well. On the other hand, *compassion* for those who have turned their backs on the moral teachings of the Lord has been more difficult for us."[2] On the many occasions I heard Van speak at a church or gathering of pastors and other ministry leaders, he always called on Christians to extend the grace of God to any who would receive it.

Van was wise enough to know, of course, that grace is not grace if not received. He did not hesitate to challenge the grace-needy person to see their part in the formula. A quote from C.S. Lewis is apropos to the subject: "St. Augustine says, 'God gives where He finds empty hands.' A man whose hands are full of parcels can't receive a gift."[3]

On occasion, someone would try to take advantage of Van's gentle spirit when they heard him speak of grace. One particular situation involved a counselee and his family. This man warmed to Van's message at church that we must offer grace to the hurting. Van had testified of his experiences and how wonderful Christian people had demonstrated the love of Christ toward him since he had turned his life over to the Lord. This man wanted that kind of acceptance. However, he would argue with Van about the wrong choices he was making. He didn't want to forsake them. He felt those things were problems for "uptight church members," but that his choices in life were just fine with God. Van sought to teach him differently. This man would sometime call early in the morning, before anyone was out of bed, or late at night, asking for help. Van was firm; he would give any help if the man would cooperate with him and begin to make important changes. The guy just didn't want to change. Van told me, "You have to give people the freedom to walk away, just as Jesus did with the rich young ruler"[4]

"Take Off Your Mask"

My son hid behind a mask for much of his life. He tried to live two lives concurrently. One was a public life where he was happy, adjusted, and doing quite well. At the same time, he was unhappy and not sure of himself at all. It had to do with sexual feelings toward male persons. How could he be interested in girls, want to marry and have a family, and fully express himself in these ways while at the same time have this strange attraction for men? He learned, he said, to live behind a mask! However, when the crisis of life and identity occurred, sick with a high fever and scared he might die, Van sobered very quickly. The teachings he had learned through the lives of his family and friends, as well as the things clearly taught in his formative years, began to surface and gain prominence in his thinking. He had a heart for God and things spiritual; that was clear to him. As he began to make deep-seated changes in his thinking, the first thing he decided to do was to be transparent. The mask he had hidden behind for so many years, formerly his protection, now became an object to loathe. His message in his sermons and conferences sounded a clear note: "Take off your mask. Life is too short and too uncertain to play games with yourself or with others. Embrace your life's story and let God bring healing and new opportunities to you. Share your life's experiences with others and trust the truth to win the day for you."

Once, in a psychology class at Houston Baptist University, Van was to present a paper before his peers and the professor. His chosen topic was "Sexual Abuse of Children and It's Devastating Potential." He shared statistics with testimonies from adult men and women who had suffered sexual abuse as children. He then, very transparently, told of his own sad, painful experiences as a child who had been sexually abused. He also acknowledged his same-sex issues

("The room was so quiet you could have heard a pin drop," he said) and the fact that he was HIV positive as a result. By this time, he said he had tears in his eyes, as did many of his classmates, as well as the teacher. Van was never proud of his story, but had learned early in his return to the Lord that embracing his history and appropriately sharing it with others was necessary for his own emotional-spiritual health, as well as a great tool for helping any who might be searching for answers.

"Forgive Yourself"

I have heard my son exhort individuals and groups of people to forgive themselves once they have squared things with the Lord and with others. He reminded us it is often easier to forgive others than to extend that same grace to yourself.

Van struggled with shame. When anyone tried to "rescue him" by minimizing the wrongness of choices he had made, he was quick to point out that for six years he knowingly and by design had chosen to follow that lifestyle. It was true he had, for a while, tried to justify his choices as natural. After all, many good people were stepping up each day to say that homosexuality was okay, and that anyone who has a problem with it or who sees it as sinful either didn't understand God or were "homophobic." Some of these people choke on the word "sin." They can find a thousand reasons to explain what has gone wrong with someone when the more appropriate explanation would be *sinful choices*.

For a short while, Van bought into that line of reasoning. However, in his heart he knew differently! Once he came to the position that he was out of step with God's will and just wanted to do his own thing, his defenses cratered on him. Guilt and shame overwhelmed him.

Van's guilt and sense of shame motivated me to think more deeply about these two subjects. In times of chatting with him about some aspect of the Christian life, he and I would discuss these issues at length. I tried to tell him that both were necessary in the healing process, but that they could be taken to an extreme. Guilt, once it has been openly and honestly dealt with before God and peers, can be dismissed from our daily thinking. God, the Bible teaches us, puts our sins away and chooses never to remember them against us.[5] Thus, guilt can be addressed on a cognitive level. The formula is simple and profound at the same time. I sin. I repent and confess (agree with God) concerning my sin. I make amends where appropriate. God forgives and even "forgets" my sin. (*A man, recently converted to the Christian faith, for a long time had had a bad habit of cursing. In a moment of anger he found himself reverting to his old habit of using profanity. To his credit, he immediately knelt down in prayer and asked the Lord's forgiveness. However, he slipped again a few days later and found himself cursing. Once more, he bowed in prayer and said, "Father, forgive me for doing it again." God replied, "Doing what again?"*) Though there may be serious consequences of my sinful choices, I am now free to put my sin out of mind and get on with my life.

Shame is related to, yet different from, guilt. It has more to do with the emotional impact on what my wrong choices have done to others or to me. It gets into one's "emotional DNA" and is a favorite tool of Satan, "the accuser of our brethren."[6] He will constantly remind a person of the terrible things done and how bad he or she must be to have participated in such unspeakable things! The focus in shame is on *feelings* and *sense of personal worth*. I once heard a speaker say, "*Guilt* is the emotional response to believing 'I **made** a mistake,' while *shame* is the emotional response to believing 'I **am** a mistake.'"[7] This feeling of unworthiness and self-disgust plagued Van. Thankfully, the longer he ministered to the needs of others and shared his own struggles with shame, the less hold it had on him.

That raises the question, however, concerning the reasons a person holds on to shame. Once there is understanding that God forgives and forgets, why do some of us choose to remember and suffer shame?

A partial explanation could be that this is one way to punish ourselves for destructive choices. The reasoning, mostly unconscious and demonic in nature, is as follows: "I messed up by making certain decisions. I've hurt many people in addition to myself and some will be scarred for life. I thank God His love and grace has forgiven me of my sin, but I don't deserve to be let off that easily.

Since neither God nor others are going to punish me, I'll do it myself by not releasing the *shame* I feel for having been so stupid."

This kind of destructive thinking usually has to be addressed over a period of time in the context of biblically-based counseling. An additional help is being part of a support group where these kinds of issues are regularly discussed and stories of freedom from guilt and shame are shared.

Another part of the process of finding freedom from shame is clearly understanding and assimilating *mercy* as a Siamese twin of *grace*. Grace is partially defined as receiving something from God I don't deserve, while mercy is <u>not</u> receiving from God something (judgment and condemnation) I <u>do</u> deserve. A heavy dose of these two Godly gifts can greatly alleviate one's need of self-punishment in the form of shame.

"Life Is Not A Dress Rehearsal"

He did not pen this "Vanism," but it certainly spoke of what was churning inside his gut. Three factors had merged in Van to become a powerful force:
- His involvement in homosexuality resulting in guilt and shame.
- The fact that he was HIV positive and constantly lived under a cloud of serious illness and probable death. Van's awareness of this threat led him to tell me on one occasion, "I have sentenced myself to a short life on the earth."
- The eagerness to make up for lost time by reaching out with a message of hope to those in pain.

These dynamic issues resulted in a sense of urgency about the brevity and uncertainty of life. Like Jonah getting a second chance to preach to the Ninevites[8], Van became a prophet, exhorting people to make wise choices in life. After he had returned to the Lord, he made another trip to see friends in Spain. In a journal he kept during that time, he wrote that one of his purposes in going was "to show my friends that I have Christ in my life."

Van became frustrated with some of his counselees because, he said, they seemed unwilling to get serious about their situations. I know of at least one time when he told a person he was not going to see him again "because you are pretending to make changes. I refuse to waste your and my time any more." That proved to be a jolt to this man and led to major adjustments in his behavior.

When I think of "Life is not a dress rehearsal," I'm reminded of a sign sitting on the desk of a pastor: "*In ten years, what do you wish you had done today? Do it now!*" The Bible sends a clear message on this subject: "Now listen, you who say, 'Today or tomorrow we will go to this or that city, spend a year there, carry on business and make money.' Why, you do not even know what will happen tomorrow. What is your life? You are a mist that appears for a little while and then vanishes. Instead, you ought to say, 'If it is the Lord's will, we will live and do this or that.'"[9]

Before his death, Van and I remembered together the shocking news we received some time earlier about a wonderful friend and deeply committed Christian, Dr. George Greener. A young medical doctor whose lifelong habit of running and other vigorous exercise, eating correctly, and seeking to live a balanced life did not save him from a massive heart attack that took his life in a moment's time. He left a wife and three young children. Recalling that event, we talked about the uncertainty of life even for those whose lifestyles are admirable. "Take the long look, the look into eternity," Van would say.

"Friends Are Important"

This boy was serious about maintaining contact with friends. It is not an exaggeration to say that, with the exception of his last four or five days, he wrote letters *every week of his life* to people he knew from high school, college, work, relatives, or others he met somewhere along the way! It was truly one of the great attributes of his life.

One thing I will always remember with great tenderness is the day he died, before he went into semi-consciousness later in the evening, he called his three nephews in Dallas to tell them he loved them. It was a touching moment for Lilly Faye, me, and Carla Faye

A Voice From Heaven

their mom, as we listened to the conversion. In their bedrooms, each has pictures and notes he had sent them.

The evening before his death, three precious children, neighbors from across the street where we live, came over with their mom to visit with Van. Their mom told us they knew Van was very sick and wanted to see him again. I peeked in the room as they stood at the foot of his bed and remember him weakly smiling at them, calling them by name and trying to acknowledge their presence.

When hearing of his death, friends from around the United States, as well as from Spain, England, Argentina, Venezuela, Mexico, and South Africa expressed their sadness, almost always referring to Van as one of their best friends!

(An interesting thing happened relative to all these friends of Van's. There were three young ladies at the memorial service, each one mentioning to my wife or me "Van was the true love of my life." Each of them referred to marriage, or having hoped that it might have happened if he had been healthy and lived. Each of the young ladies had been his friend for many years.)

Another story that surfaced at the time of Van's death was an exchange between a young lady who had been in high school with Van. Now living and working in New York, this girl said that she was something of a "loner" in high school and that Van had gone out of his way on more than one occasion to speak to her and to ask about things of interest to her. At a high school ten-year reunion, Van had danced several times with her. She let us know very clearly that, though their paths had gone separate ways after high school, she would always consider Van one of the most important persons she had known.

There are other "Vanisms" listed below. Lilly Faye and I have printed bookmarks that contain a list of some of them. They include:

"Leave a Legacy"

"Tell Your Own Story"

"Family Is Important"

"God is more concerned about your character than He is about your comfort"

A Voice From Heaven

The quote most unique to Van, and referred to by many people, was his statement: "God gives do-overs." The night he told his story before eight hundred people at the First Baptist Church in Katy, he referred to the time when he played on his high school tennis team. He said that it was their custom, when warming up at the beginning of their games, to give each other "do-overs." He said that it was the equivalent of a "mulligan" in golf. He likened this to the grace of God who gives second chances to people after they have messed up.

Van loved to encourage his counselees or others in his messages by pointing to God's "do-overs." Since he was a recipient of this grace and God had given him another chance, it was something of which my son <u>never</u> lost sight!! When he preached or spoke of it, it was always with great excitement.

One day about a year after Van had gone to heaven, we received a telephone call from a gentleman. The conversion went something like this: "Hello. May I speak with Van Wisdom please?" I was a little shaken by the request, but replied, "Van passed away about a year ago. Who is calling, please?"

"Oh no!" said the man. "I'm so sorry. I didn't know. Are you Van's dad?" I told him I was. He continued, "We don't know each other, Mr. Wisdom, but I just heard Van's testimony on tape and was compelled to call. This morning, my car would not start so I borrowed my mother-in law's car. There was a tape in the deck and I decided to check it out, thinking perhaps it was music. When I began listening to Van tell how God has worked in his life, I was deeply touched. Mr. Wisdom, I have had serious problems with drugs and alcohol the past three or four years. I felt there was no hope for me; I had ruined my life and I was traveling on a dead-end street." At this juncture, he began to cry. I listened, somewhat in shock, as he continued, "I know now that God was sending me a message through Van. When I heard him talk of having a God who gives us "do-overs," it seemed as though the Lord was speaking directly to me!! Hope for a second chance to do what is right welled up in me! I called my mother-in-law and asked how I could get in touch with Van. She did not know him personally, but knew he was from the First Baptist Church in Katy and would find the number for me. That's when I called you."

Now, I was the one crying. Especially when he said, "Mr. Wisdom, you can know that *even though your son has died, his influence is still living!*"

Dear Wisdoms,

I just wanted you to know that I remember you everyday in my prayers and I think of Van and smile. The Easter Sunday Service at my church was about God giving "Do-Overs." I know in my heart that Van was standing next to my pastor whispering in his ear "This one's for her." As the pastor marched out after the eulogy, he leaned over and squeezed my arm—he knew too.

Thank you for sharing your love and acceptance with so many of us over the years. Van was able to live the life that he did and share so much of himself because you stood beside him.

P.J.

Dear Uncle Charles and Aunt Lilly Faye,

I am so privileged to have known Van and to have had him as a part of my life. His life was living proof of God's mercy and the perfect plan He has for our lives. We are all told this in church, but Van proved with his life that they are not empty words, but words full of meaning and of promise.

He was so proud of his family and of your grace and strength during this season of hardship. He was safe and secure in your unconditional love for him. Your loving care of Van was such a testimony of how Jesus wants us to be. I know God must be sending you tender mercies in the same measure that you gave to Van.

Van will be missed by so many—I still have trouble believing he's gone. But I think he is sending us little bits from heaven—as we were leaving church on Sunday I heard a little boy say to his mom, "It was so nice of God to give us sunshine today"—and it made me smile — —What a Van thing to say!

All my love,
BEV

Dear Charles,

The Lord has put you on my heart all day Saturday and Sunday to pray for you. Please tell Lilly Faye that of all the funerals and memorial services that I have been to (including those I have done), Van's was the most glorifying to the Lord and honoring of the loved one, that I have ever witnessed. The truth was spoken in love in so many ways.

What a testimony to our "Mulligan God"! You truly heard from God in how you handled the service. For Van to come back to the Lord, you and Lilly Faye's and the Lord's love must have been continually unconditional and over whelming. O that the church would love like that.

I wanted to be at your service Sunday morning to pray for you, but Gary asked me to preach. I look forward to getting the tape and listening to it. I know you have several pastors you meet with regularly to pray for our city and one another, but if you'd like prayer or a word of encouragement or a listening ear please call me. I'd love to minister back to you.

May the Lord bless you and Lilly Faye with His wonderful love and presence as you seek his grace!

Your friend and co-laborer in the Lord,
L.S.

CHAPTER 8 — "THOUGH HE IS DEAD, HE IS STILL SPEAKING..."

(This message was delivered to the 2002 Graduating Class of Houston Baptist University. Commencement was held in Houston's First Baptist Church in May 2002)

Hebrew 11:4

Thank you President Hodo for the honor of speaking to the graduates of Houston Baptist University.

I congratulate each of you and your family members as you reach this milestone in your life. This is a great day, but it is the prayer and expectation of all of us that your greatest days are yet ahead of you.

In the book of Hebrews in the New Testament, chapter eleven is known as "The Hall Of Fame" of great saints. In verses 4 and 5, we are told that the great faith of Abel served him well and the latter part of that passage reads, "By faith he still speaks, even though he is dead."

My brief challenge to each of the graduates this morning is as follows: live your life in such a way that you maximize your possibilities and, when you die, it will be said of you "He/she is still speaking." May you so impact your world that even after death, your influence is still felt.

A Voice From Heaven

As Dr. Hodo said to you a few minutes ago, our son died two months ago. If he had lived, he would have walked across this stage with you today receiving his Master Of Arts In Psychology Degree with you. My wife and I, along with our two daughters and their families, are so grateful to Dr. Hodo, the faculty, and administration of the university who have posthumously conferred that degree upon Van. In a small way, even that act is an indication that, *being dead, he is still speaking!*

Without being morbid on the day of your university graduation, I want to share with you about our son, Van. His story is sad, yet ends on a beautiful note.

When he was a little boy, Van was sexually abused. He chose not to tell us or anyone else about that traumatic time in his life until a few years after his graduation from college. Throughout his years of public education, Van was, seemingly, a well-adjusted and happy kid. According to his own words, however, he was engaged in serious inner conflict.

After finishing college, Van moved to Spain to live and work. While there, largely because of his struggles with sexual identity issues resulting from the trauma of abuse as a child, he became involved in homosexual activities. Time limitations do not allow me to give you details of how his deep, dark secret kept him in turmoil. After four years of that lifestyle, he unfortunately became infected with the HIV virus. During that time, he ran away from God, from his family, and he tried to run away from himself. Thank God, the pull of family love and his love for Jesus Christ eventually brought him back home to all of us. The last five or six years, he has been in ministry, involved in a life that I have chosen to describe as "the greatest tragedy becoming the greatest triumph." He was given leadership in a ministry to persons who struggle with issues of brokenness in their lives, giving him opportunity to speak in the Houston area as well as places around the world like England, Israel, and South America.

For our family, his death has been very painful. Yet we believe that through the people he has touched in testimony, speaking, counseling, and in a ministry he started called New Beginnings, *being dead, he is still speaking!* On this earth, his influence is very much alive! God's grace and providential methods can bring forth miraculous results in amazing ways!

Last weekend, our family was together in Dallas. A young man who is part of the family, a distant relative, had dropped out of college 12 years ago. He told me, after coming to the memorial service, he had been profoundly impacted by Van's testimony. "I'm going back to college; I want to finish what I started a long time ago. I wanted you and Mrs. Wisdom to know that it was because of Van I am impressed that this is what I need to do."

Being dead, he is still speaking!

A young lady who had been close to Van from the time they were in elementary school, and had graduated from Baylor University with him, wrote us from her home in New York City last week: "Uncle Charles and Aunt Lilly Faye, I attended church yesterday and I heard something I want to share with the two of you. As you know, Van often spoke of God giving us a "do-over"—giving us a second chance. My pastor spoke on this theme and even used the term "do-over" in his sermon. I was so sad as I thought about Van. In that moment, however, I felt as though I saw Van standing next to the pastor, smiling at me. After the sermon, as the pastor walked up the aisle to the front door to greet people, passing near me on the aisle, he gently reached down and touched my shoulder. It was like Van was saying to me, 'Jennifer, be encouraged. The Lord will give all of us a 'do-over' when we need it.'"

Being dead, he is still speaking!

One last story before I finish. The day of the memorial service, our plans were to have a family gathering at the graveside and let relatives and other loved ones share testimonies about Van. The public service was to be held in the early afternoon in the worship center of the First Baptist Church of Katy. That morning, however, the weather was very cold and winds were gusting at twenty to twenty-five miles an hour. Hank Schmidt, friend and owner of Schmidt Funeral Home in Katy, came to me with the suggestion that our family have the private service in the chapel at the funeral home. Hank told me, "Don't worry about the burial; I will personally see to the interment while you, family, and friends have your time together." We followed Mr. Schmidt's recommendation and had a wonderful time, sharing memories of Van.

Later, the family had lunch together at the church, and just before it was time for the memorial service to begin, I went to my study to meditate. After a few minutes there was a knock on my door. I called for the person to come in and it was Mr. Schmidt. He said to me with great tenderness in his voice and tears in his eyes, "Charles, I've taken care of the burial." In that moment, my mind went back forty years earlier when I was a seminary student. A speaker in chapel had made this statement (and I had not thought of it in many years), "Live your life in such a way that when you die, even the funeral director will cry." When I saw Hank Schmidt's tears, I thanked God for the impression that our son had on him as well. Being dead, he is still speaking!

Young adults, I am fully aware, however, that this day is not about Van Wisdom. It is about you! You are right to be excited about your graduation and eager to face the challenges of life ahead of you. The prayers of this university will join the prayers of your families in asking God to maximize your opportunities. We long for each of you the most fulfilling life possible. I specifically will ask God to help you so live that, even many years hence, when you die, you will still be speaking!

Thank you.

Dear Dr. and Mrs. Wisdom,

This has strangely been the best and worst of times. To not have Van sitting beside me at HBU graduation was painful. Although I know with certainty that he has graduated to a much higher place. Van was pure sunshine in my life and I will always remember his love and craziness! We were both pretty adolescent at times...but had such a good time together. I will treasure those memories.

G.R.

Dear Dr. and Mrs. Wisdom,

I was so very sad to read of your sweet son's death. He and I were classmates at HBU, and there was something very extraordinary and special about him. I'll miss Van. I know he is with Christ—but I'll miss him here.

MM

CHAPTER 9—SERMONS FROM THE HEART

"The Prodigal Son"
(June 1999)

Charles

Van and I are sharing the pulpit this Father's Day, and our topic is the well-known parable, "The Prodigal Son."

I think most, if not all, of you heard Van's testimony to the church about a year ago. If you have not (or have) and would like a tape of it, please call the church office and request one. Having heard him share his story with the church will give you a fuller appreciation of what he and I have to say in this message.

Van

Please stand with me for the reading of God's word. We are in Luke, chapter 15, starting at verse ll.
11. Jesus continued: "There was a man who had two sons.
12. The younger one said to his father, 'Father, give me my share of the estate.' So he divided his property between them.

13. Not long after that, the younger son got together all he had, set off for a distant country and there squandered his wealth in wild living.

14. After he had spent everything, there was a severe famine in that whole country, and he began to be in need.

15. So he went and hired himself out to a citizen of that country, who sent him to his fields to feed pigs.

16. He longed to fill his stomach with the pods that the pigs were eating, but no one gave him anything.

17. When he came to his senses, he said, 'How many of my father's hired men have food to spare, and here I am starving to death!

18. I will set out and go back to my father and say to him: Father, I have sinned against heaven and against you.

19. I am no longer worthy to be called your son; make me like one of your hired men.'

20. So he got up and went to his father. But while he was still a long way off, his father saw him and was filled with compassion for him; he ran to his son, threw his arms around him and kissed him.

21. The son said to him, 'Father, I have sinned against heaven and against you. I am no longer worthy to be called your son.

22. But the father said to his servants, 'Quick! Bring the best robe and put it on him. Put a ring on his finger and sandals on his feet.

23. Bring the fattened calf and kill it. Let's have a feast and celebrate.

24. For this son of mine was dead and is alive again; he was lost and is found.' So they began to celebrate."

Charles

It has been said that the parable of the Prodigal Son is the most beautiful story ever told. It certainly is a rich story. Van and I have been studying it all week in preparation for today, yet we know we'll not begin to scratch the surface of all that is to be found. There are wonderful insights into human nature and the nature of God. Specifically, there is much to learn of the nature of sin, the need of repentance, and the forgiveness of God.

Here is the direction we'll take in sharing this story with you:

I. The Appeal of What is "Out There"
   A. There is Feasting
   B. There is Famine

II. The Appeal of Home
   A. The Road Back Home
   B. The Welcome Back Home

The Great Appeal of What is "Out There"

A definition of *prodigal* is a good place to start. "Wastefully extravagant or reckless" is what one dictionary calls it.[1] How did this happen in the life of this seemingly good family?

When we first look at the story, we see the family intact and at home. There is no mention of a mother; perhaps she has died. If so, this father must have had his hands full raising two seemingly strong-willed sons. Yet, perhaps he felt everything was running smoothly. There seems to be no obvious reason why the family is about to be severely tested.

Many families look great on the surface. The truth is, as every parent can testify, more often than not, there is some kind of crisis brewing in the home, often just below the surface.

The younger son is restless. Perhaps unknown to the father, as well as to the busy older brother, this boy is dreaming of places "out there." "Surely," he says to himself, "there is more to life than the hum-drum pattern around this farm!" It is the thinking that is based in reality, but almost always blown out of proportion to what is factual. It's an attractive and effective ploy of the Christian's arch-enemy, Satan. "There is a place 'out there,'" he whispers, "that offers so much more than what you're experiencing. 'Out there' are plenty of fun people, exciting adventures, and the deeply satisfying sensual pleasures that have been *unfairly* kept away from you. Your father and older brother are good people, we admit that, but they just don't know how to really live. 'Out there,' you'll surpass them by having so much fun, they will probably even wish they were in your place."

The "out there" picture looks so good! Once a person latches on to those kinds of thoughts, it is only a matter of time before they find a way to move in that direction. I read somewhere that the *lust* was in the prodigal's heart long before *dust* of the far country was on his feet.

Van

It dawned on me yesterday, while thinking about this message, that this guy had been planning on "escaping" the family for some time. It was not a sudden thought or behavior. Verse 12 says he asked his father for an early distribution of the estate. That was unusual; estate inheritance does not usually occur until the death of the parents. (Tax lawyers in the congregation will probably disagree with the practice of this tradition.) Then, verse 13 says, "Not long after that, the younger son.... left."

The prodigal son did not interpret his eagerness for what was "out there" as turning his back on his family as much as he felt it was time for him to "spread his wings." I know that when I left home, it was only after giving a lot of thought to it, working hard to save the necessary money, and planning on the right place to go to find my "out there" world. Though part of my motive in moving to Spain was to protect my parents from pain of a son who was making disappointing decisions, it was never in my heart to completely cut my parents and sisters out of my life.

Charles

At this juncture, let me personalize this story somewhat from a father's perspective. As most of you know, the father in the parable represents God while the two sons represent those of us who are members of His family.

We know the prodigal son's father did no wrong in this story. In fact, he did everything right. God can do no wrong!

However, there are fathers who may contribute to the decisions their prodigal sons make. I have struggled on many occasions as I wondered about the ways I failed Van and inadvertently pushed him toward a prodigal lifestyle. Did I neglect him at crucial times of his life? One painful question that has run through my mind is, "Why did

Van not come to me when he was sexually abused? Was I too busy for him? Was I insensitive and better at *talking to him* than I was at *listening and dialoguing with him*?

It is a hard pill for a father to swallow to think maybe he contributed to his son's prodigal life!

Van

I appreciate what you are saying, Dad, and every father knows he probably could have done a better job at parenting. It is not my job to absolve you and any other father of what you feel is an issue you have to deal with in your assessment of life.

However, I will have to take responsibility for the decisions I made as an adult. No one forced me to go the places I went or do the things I did. Those were my choices.

Feasting

This boy was not disappointed when he first arrived in the distant land. With the money and eagerness he possessed, it was easy to find lots of "friends" who would help him spend his dough! "Wine, women, and song" filled his days and nights for the first few months he was there. He had definitely made the right decision! Poor Dad and Older Brother, sweating bullets on the farm; they just did not know what they were missing!

Make no mistake about it: there is lots of fun in the distant land! Parties seem to multiply in abundance and people come out of the walls to spend time with you. You are the star of the party!

The church at times has not taken seriously the strong attraction of living in a prodigal world! We have, rightly, jumped to the problems associated with this sort of living. However, we underestimate the magnetic pull of the sordid life! Why else would fathers and mothers desert their families? How do you explain the unquenchable hunger for more and more of the "fast-lane" living that sucks new multitudes into its path each day? The entertainment world throws at our youth message after message, many of them subliminal, that they have not truly experienced life until they imitate the lifestyles, dress, and behavior of Hollywood and professional athletes.

I thought I had truly "arrived" when I first went to Barcelona, Spain. It took just a few days until I found attractive and fun-loving young adults from around the world who were living the "good life."

Let it be said clearly: there is *feasting* in the land of the prodigal.

However, that is not all there is in the distant land! That is just "phase one" of a much-detailed story.

Famine

Verse 14 tells us that the entire country was plagued with a severe famine. As a result, now that he had used up his money, the prodigal lost his friends. Moreover, he lost his self-respect. To survive, he went to work on a hog farm. If you know much about Orthodox Jewish teaching, you know that pigs were off-limits to the Jews. It was the lowest of the low for this young man to work on the pig farm, slopping the pigs. What cold reality that the feast was over! In addition, what painful results of choosing the prodigal path!

Charles

If you note closely, the fifteenth chapter of Luke is really about *three* lost, "prodigal" entities: the lost sheep in verses 3-7, the lost coin in verses 8-10, and the lost son in these verses we are studying. There is a common thread running through all of them: they are all lost and there is suffering as a result.

The lost sheep just wanders away, following one juicy patch after another, while at the same time moving further and further away from the protection of the fold and the shepherd.

The lost coin is valueless. As long as the coin is lost, what needs can it supply? What is worse, it cannot bleat like the sheep or come to its senses like the son. It is in a hopeless situation unless someone takes the initiative to come looking for it.

The lost son is miserable. The fleeting joy of the *feast* exaggerates the pain of the famine.

The boy's pain is greater than it might be under other circumstances. If he had fallen on hard times because he was making right decisions, yet ran into calamity, the pain would be there, but not as great. He is in a pigpen because of selfish and foolish choices.

Three lost valuables: a sheep, a coin, and a son. One is astray, one in helpless, and one is foolish. They all have this in common, however: there is *misery* in being lost.

Van

I'm the one to testify to that truth. In Spain I immediately found lots of friends, and the parties were exciting. There were people from Sweden, Germany, England, France, and, of course, Spain in our group.

I'm always amazed at how quickly money can disappear. As mentioned earlier, I had saved some money before I left for Europe. It went fast, however. Thankfully, I did not have to slop pigs to make a little money. I was fortunate to find a nice family who gave me a small bedroom in the back of their house. I taught English a couple of hours a day, but it was never enough to really sustain me. Besides that, I was going skiing in France and spending time on the beach in Southern Spain; who wanted to work when they could do those fun things?

In my heart, however, I was miserable. I missed my family. I missed the many good things I had back home. At first, my pride would not allow me to tell them how lonely and truly unhappy I was during that time. Thank God, He gave me strength to save enough money to make the trip home!

Charles

Someone has said that life is ordered in such a way that we cannot see the consequences of our choices. When we choose a path, we choose its end! The Bible warns us that Christians have an enemy who blinds them. The results are often sad.

The Appeal of Home

History is filled with stories of men and women who have yielded to the darker side of their nature, come to realize they are on the wrong track, and find the right path. That is true of our hero in this story. Note the three aspects of the return:
1. Awareness
2. Acknowledgement
3. Action

Listen to the words of verse 17: "When he came to his senses…" It's like the poor boy had taken leave of his senses when he walked away from his father.

To live one's life as though there is no God is foolish. Scripture, an "inner voice," and many other "witnesses" constantly remind us that there is Someone greater than us in the universe. When we intentionally put that aside and determine we're going to live life as though God does not exist, we embrace a senseless posture!

However, to his credit, this young man came to his senses. It's like one day he "woke up" and saw things as they really were.

In 1972-1973, I was a chaplain intern at the Texas Research Institute of Mental Sciences in the Medical Center of Houston. Many of our patients were out of touch with reality. For whatever reason, they escaped from the world of reality and lived in some kind of fantasy. However, when they began to regain their mental health (and many of these came about as people found peace with the Lord, I'm happy to say), one of the first things we would note about them was they had reconnected with reality. They were aware of where they were and why they had landed there in the first place. They were then in a position to make the necessary changes to gain emotional strength and get on with their lives. You might say they "woke up" and saw things as they really are.

Van

Then, in verses 17 and 18 he says, "How many of my father's hired men have food to spare and here I am starving to death. I will set out and go back to my father and say to him: 'Father, I have sinned against heaven and against you.'" The prodigal son became aware of his deplorable situation and, credit to him, acknowledged his foolish choices.

My return home started with my coming home from Spain. However, it was some time later that I realized I had done more than just being foolish when I left for Spain. I had sinned against God, my father, and my family. That was not, unfortunately, until after I learned I had cancer. With my compromised immune condition due to the HIV situation, I was really scared! I may not have slopped pigs, but I doubt I could have felt lower in those times until in my heart I abandoned the "far country" and returned to the Lord and to my loved ones.

There was one more important step the prodigal had to take. Action was needed. To this point, it was all mental and emotional. That was good, but until you and I put feet to our thoughts, we'll just remain in the first phase of our return.

To keep the application personal, let me share what that involved for me. Dad and I had been talking about the need of my sharing my story with the entire church. Boy, was that a toughie!! I guess I wanted to come home, but to "slip in the back door." While I rejected the idea in the beginning (my pride was yelling at me to protect myself), I softened when I saw the kind of response Dad and Mom were getting as they told our family's story in the small groups of twenty to twenty-five people. I guess you can say the Lord spoke to my heart and gave me the encouragement I needed.

The night I gave my testimony at the church (when we were in the old location), I was as nervous as I had ever been in my life. I looked out over the packed house that night and saw members of this church, many community leaders, pastors from other churches, friends, and family members. Wow! I just didn't know if I could do it. However, God gave me the strength and I can honestly say that is the night I *fully* came home! (*Applause*)

Charles

That was one of the true highlights of our family's life. To see how God spoke through Van. I sensed his struggle and humility before the

Lord and the world. But, it was truly a "God thing" as the Holy Spirit moved mightily in our midst and hundreds of folks came forward that night to pray with Van and staff members.

What about the welcome home? Did it go well? What can you and I expect when we have been prodigal sons and come back to the Lord and our spiritual family?

Unfortunately, some do not like it! It's hard to realize there are "elder sons" who will resent the prodigal and not rejoice in his return. A couple of guesses as to why:

- Maybe they doubt the sincerity of the prodigal's return.
- Perhaps they are angry for the way the prodigal hurt his father, or the family reputation.
- Unfortunately, some "elder sons" serve the father faithfully, but with joyless hearts. Like the Pharisees of Jesus' day, they go through all the motions out of habit rather than love for the father. These people are unable to rejoice in the rising again of one who is fallen; all they can do is focus on the fall.

Van

Let me be quick to say that almost 100%, this church and the people of this community, like my family, have been overwhelming in their love and support of me. It is much, much more generous than I could ever have hoped for.

Charles

Let's move quickly to the real hero of this parable: the father. He did so many right things in welcoming his son home. Consider the following:

- "While he was still a long way off, his father saw him" (v.20). The father was actually looking for his son. Can this convey anything but his longing for the boy? Can't you see the old man walking out on the porch several times a day, looking up the road the boy took when he left home?

- "He was filled with compassion for him"(v.20). Any anger, disappointment, or compulsion to discipline or lecture the boy was swallowed up in his love for his son.

The gist of this entire chapter on the lost sheep, the lost coin, and the lost son is that God saves men and He does so because He wishes and delights to do so!

Van

If you are here today and you feel alienated from God, from a family member or anyone of importance to you, things can change for the good. Learn from the prodigal son. Learn from my experiences as well. I can assure you, it is much more blessed and satisfying to be home than it is to live out there in the "distant land." Trust me; God will do something beautiful in your life.
(At this juncture, Van and the choir of the First Baptist Church, Katy, begin to sing, "Something Beautiful.")

"The Prodigal Father"
(June 2000)

Van

Last year, Dad and I started a tradition of presenting the sermon together on Father's Day. Last year, the sermon was on the Prodigal Son. This year, we decided to preach about the Prodigal Father. *(Van is smiling at me in a kind of "getting even time" manner.)*

Charles

Men, we just don't get any respect, do we? For instance, do you know that we receive on Father's Day just a pittance of the attention that is given to mothers on Mother's Day? The phone companies say that the long-distance calls on Father's Day are half as many as are long distance calls on Mother's Day. (By the way, many of those are collect, I might add!)

Van

I think I made a few of those also.

Charles

I think that is correct!

Van

Our scripture reading for today is Genesis 37:1-11. Would you please stand while I read this passage?

Genesis 37: 1-11

1. Jacob lived in the land where his father had stayed, the land of Canaan.

2. This is the account of Jacob. Joseph, a young man of seventeen, was tending the flocks with his brothers, the sons of Bilhah and the sons of Zilpah, his father's wives, and he brought their father a bad report about them.

3. Now Israel loved Joseph more than any of his other sons, because he had been born to him in his old age; and he made a richly ornamented robe for him.

4. When his brothers saw that their father loved him more than any of them, they hated him and could not speak a kind word to him.

5. Joseph had a dream, and when he told it to his brothers, they hated him all the more.

6. He said to them, "Listen to this dream I had:

7. We were binding sheaves of grain out in the field when suddenly my sheaf rose and stood upright, while your sheaves gathered around mine and bowed down to it."

8. His brothers said to him, "Do you intend to reign over us? Will you actually rule us?" And they hated him all the more because of his dream and what he had said.

9. Then he had another dream, and he told it to his brothers, "Listen," he said, "I had another dream, and this time the sun and moon and eleven stars were bowing down to me."

10. When he told his father as well as his brothers, his father rebuked him and said, "What is this dream you had? Will your mother and I and your brothers actually come and bow down to the ground before you?"

11. His brothers were jealous of him, but his father kept the matter in mind.

Charles

We have an outline that will help all of us stay on target. It is printed on the screen:

> I. MAN'S REALITY: THE BAD NEWS
>   A. *Preferential Parenting*
>   B. *Perpetual Parenting*
>   C. *Passive Parenting*
>
> II. GOD'S REALITY: THE GOOD NEWS
>   A. God Reacts
>   B. God Reconciles
>   C. God Rewards

A Voice From Heaven

Van

The story of Joseph is one of great interest to many people. It is certainly one of the most beautiful stories in the Old Testament. I have always been interested in it if for no other reason than my middle name is Joseph, Dad's middle name is Joseph, and my grandfather's middle name was Joseph.

Here it is in summary fashion: Joseph was the seventeen-year-old son of Jacob and Rachel. He is referred to as Joseph's favorite son because he was born to Jacob and Rachel when they were advanced in years. When we are first introduced to him, he gives the impression of being brash. "Too big for his own britches," we might say.

Three things happen that create serious problems in a family where there is already tension. The first is when Joseph brings his father, Jacob, a negative report about his brothers.

The second thing that happened to cause a wall to develop between Joseph and his brothers was when Jacob made a coat of many colors for his obviously favorite son.

Then, when Joseph told his brothers about his dreams, which depicted a time was coming when they would bow down to him. Well, that was the proverbial "straw that broke the camel's back." After that, "they could not speak a kind word to him."

Fast forward to some time later when the brothers, seething over the growing hatred for Joseph, decide to kill him. Instead of doing that, they sell him to a caravan of traders passing through the country, headed south to Egypt.

In Egypt, Joseph is sold on the auction block to Potiphar, the captain of Pharaoh's guard. With a strong faith in God, hard work and developing the leadership qualities with which God had endowed him, Joseph quickly becomes a trusted servant in Potiphar's household.

All is not well at home, however. Potiphar's wife tries to seduce the young Hebrew slave and when he rejects her, she lies about him. Joseph is sent to prison.

At this juncture, let's remind ourselves that too many of us would complain to God. It would go something like this: "God, I'm trying to make the most of a bad situation. I have not rejected You even though You've allowed me to fall into some pretty deep holes the past few years. I've been faithful to You and my reward is prison."

Joseph, however, is not like that. Instead, he begins the same hard work, strong faith in God, and exercising the leadership gifts the Lord has bestowed on him. Guess what? Before long, he is the leading prisoner in jail!

Long story short is that Joseph eventually has a chance to help the top man himself, Pharaoh. For that, he is rewarded with a very responsible position in the government. Before long, he is number two man in the land!

Like me, you've probably heard people say, "When life gives you a lemon, turn it into lemonade." That is precisely what Joseph did with his very bad circumstances. It's a beautiful story of "from the pit to the palace!"

Charles

Then the big climax that takes us back to the beginning of the story: Joseph's brothers actually do bow before him as they come to Egypt looking for food. It is a beautiful story of forgiveness and restoration among family members.

Let's go to the first point as we glean lessons from this account.

Man's Reality: The Bad News

Since this message is part two of last year's sermon about The Prodigal Son, we have to look at The Prodigal Father. We refer, of course, to Jacob.

Jacob's shortcomings as a father evolved around three types of parenting.

The first is *preferential parenting*. By that, I refer to openly showing favoritism to young Joseph. It might be understandable—an old man has a child when he thinks he will never have children again. However, it was really insensitive of the old man to openly demonstrate his preference for Joseph in front of the others. It is amazing that so much heartache could come to this family through such a seemingly small thing.

To the child left out, however, it is no small thing. Novels have been written and movies made about sibling rivalry because one was the favorite of Mom or Dad. Moreover, I have counseled many families who have suffered hell on earth because of this kind of behavior.

Van

Dad, I read this week an additional observation about this favoritism malady. D. Stuart Briscoe writes in *The Communicator's Commentary,* "When parents insist on spoiling their children they make it very difficult for those same children to grow up mature and complete. Joseph had to deal with negative peer pressure as well as unhelpful parental pressure."[2] Joseph, in time, had to overcome the ill effects of his hateful brothers as well as the negative effects of a doting father.

Charles

The bottom line, fathers and grandfathers, is that we may inadvertently set the stage for serious difficulties for our kids if we show partiality.

The next type of parenting that can result in painful experiences in a family, one of which every mom and dad must be aware, is *perpetual parenting*. We're referring to what the Bible calls "the sins of the fathers,"[3] or generational sins. This is when one generation in a family perpetuates the wrong that was committed by the generation(s) preceding it.

It is interesting that Jacob had been part of a dysfunctional family where his parents, Isaac and Rebekah, had shown favoritism to him and his twin brother, Esau.[4] That kind of behavior had resulted in the two boys hating each other for years and Esau vowing to kill Jacob. Jacob was driven from his home for twenty years and though there was reconciliation, there was always tension between the brothers.

Did Jacob learn his lesson? No! He turned around and did the very same thing in his family.

Allow me to shift gears and tell you how this particular malady has had negative impact in my own family.

One of the issues Van and I have discussed with each other, and in some of our sessions with a Christian counselor, is my lack of time spent with him at crucial times of his life. When Van and the girls were small, I felt as though I was spending lots of quality time with them. I was diligent to go to every school event in which they participated and met with every one of the teachers they ever had for progress reports. As a family, we went to ball games at school, movies, and I felt we spent lots of time together as a family. I helped coach his Little League baseball team,

However, I know now that Van and I "missed each other" in some way or the other when he needed me badly. It dawned on me one day when the two of us were in a session with our counselor that I had spent many a day caring for the kids of other families and somehow or the other had neglected my own son! It has been very painful for me to even think about it, much less hear myself saying the words out loud.

As you can imagine, this is something that has gone over and over in my mind the past few years. As I've pondered it, I've come to an important insight. It does not make my failures any more acceptable, but it has helped make sense of things for me.

My dad's father died when he was very young, around four or five. My dad never really knew his father. Since his mother, my grandmother, never remarried, Dad never had a father in his home. He did have some older brothers, fortunately, and they helped care for the family. But a father never parented him.

When Mom and Dad married and I came along as the second child, first son in the family, my dad was absent much of my life. He was captain of a tugboat and worked two weeks away from home, then would be home for a few days. Most of those times, especially in his pre-Christian days when he was younger, he developed a serious drinking problem. Obviously, that did not sit well with my mother and sparks flew between them, leading him to stay away from home even more. The point is, my father was an "absent" father the first twelve to fourteen years of my life. He never threw a ball to me, never went with me to a ball game or to a movie, never held a tennis racquet in his hand. When I graduated from high school and, later, college (seminary also), my dad was not there. I coped by saying to myself, "Dad has to work hard to take care of our family." I guess I just tried to make the most of it. I did not doubt my father's love, just his involvement in my daily life.

I came along and have parented much as my father had parented me. This is called "generational sins."

Dad, you may love your child more than you love your life. But as someone has said, the best way to spell the four-letter word *love* is "T-I-M-E." It takes time to really bond with your child and develop an emotional closeness. Doing things together, finding time to sit down and talk about important issues, giving of yourself without looking at your watch: these are all great ways to demonstrate love and care for your son or daughter. All this simply takes a great deal of time.

Van

Believe me Dad, coming to understand what you have just explained has helped me see things more clearly since we have had these kinds of talks the past few years.

Passive parenting is the third type of parenting that may cause major pain in a family. This is when moms or dads (more prevalent among dads) simply refuse to get involved in the life of the child.

Men are guiltier of this because of two or three reasons. For one, by nature, the mother is the caregiver since she carries the baby for nine months and then gives detailed attention to the helpless infant. Societal expectations underscore the fact that the mom is going to spend much more time with the child than the dad.

Additionally, men are project-oriented by nature. We set goals, decide on four or five steps we need to take to reach that goal, then lose ourselves in the process (often giving more of our time and attention to our work or project than we do to our family).

When there are sticky, interpersonal problems in the family, men prefer to not get involved. When is the last time you saw a dad tenderly handling a small child who is screaming at the top of his or her lungs? Fewer times than when we see mom in the same situation. Moms don't withdraw from those kinds of scenarios; they plunge headfirst into whatever is going on. Not dads. A project we can fix; an emotional relationship mess-up scares us. So, in family happenings, we lean heavily in the direction of passivity.

I think we can see some of this in Jacob's family. He seemed unaware of the tension between the older boys and Joseph. He could have said, "Son, I see things are messed up here. I don't know the answer; what is your opinion of what is going on?"

Don't miss an important point here. Kids know a lot concerning the cause of the trouble when things are not working as they should. If you can maintain communication with your children, they will be able to help more than you can imagine. To do it, you have to encourage dialogue with your kids.

There was a time when I first returned home from Spain that Dad and I agreed we would meet once a week at a certain restaurant halfway between my job and the church. I thought that was a grand idea and looked forward to each Thursday's reunion. However, it did not take long for me to realize I was a "project" for him. He was, I fully understand, concerned about my walk with the Lord and how I was using my time. On the other hand, I wanted to spend time with Dad, to "hang-out," as the kids say. I just wanted to be his son, to be loved and have an adult-to-adult relationship with him.

As a result, I found more and more ready excuses for not being able to meet him on those Thursdays. He, of course, picked up on my attitude and it led to more frustration between the two of us. I clearly remember an occasion where we "agreed to disagree" and allow God and time to work out the details of our relationship.

That's what most kids want from their dad: a relationship. I think it is Josh McDowell whose quote makes lots of sense when he exhorts parents, dads in particular, to be aware of how they are relating to their kids, especially if the kids are teenagers or older. He says, "Rules without relationship will lead to rebellion."[5]

Charles

Fathers, Van has spoken with wisdom (no pun intended). Passivity is a curse in the lives of many men.

However, let me come to the "rescue" of dads just a little. A major reason we are passive in times of trouble is, often, *we just don't know what to do!* When Lilly Faye and I first learned of Van's abuse as a child, our first response was one of guilt. Why had we not protected our son? Then, learning of the resulting struggle he had with his male identity and choices he had made the last year of college, we were in a stupor! Lastly, there was the devastating news that he was HIV positive. We wept a lot and prayed. I did what I do best; I "preached" at him and called him to repent and seek help. However, the devil used our pride as Christian leaders, telling us to beat ourselves up with accusations. "How can you be a pastor, teach and preach about God's plan for the family, yet fail so miserably? No one will want you as pastor of their church when they learn how you have neglected your son!"

Dads, seek help. Don't let your pride keep you from saying to someone in whom you have confidence, "What do I do? What counsel and help can you give me?" I've learned across the years that fear of looking weak is a ploy of Satan to keep us from getting the help we so desperately need. The truth is, the Bible strongly encourages us to lean on one another and give assistance to a brother or sister who is in some kind of trouble.[6] Until we do, we are going to be miserable. Foolishness causes us to say to ourselves, "I can work this out by myself. I'll just keep on going forward as though nothing is wrong and surely some kind of answer will materialize."

Lilly Faye and I sought guidance from a Christian counselor and he helped a great deal. A while later, I told a pastor friend. I shared with him we had decided to resign the church, move to another community, and I would get a job doing something else. His response seemed to be words that came directly out of heaven: "Don't even consider that! The devil wants you to run; stand up to Him! Tell your story, with Van's approval of course, to the closest friends you have in the church and community. Let God's family give you the support you need. We pastors think we are only to *give help* and fail to see our need to *receive help*. Charles, you and Lilly Faye need help; go get it."

Dads, if you don't know what to do, seek help. Do it quickly!

God's Reality: The Good News

Van

Let's shift gears and focus on the Lord. We've got problems; no doubt. However, God has solutions! He never leaves us in our time of need.

The hopeful part of this story of Joseph, his father, and his brothers is that God responded in three specific ways. He responds with us in the same way.

1. God reacts.
2. God reconciles.
3. God rewards.

Charles

Thank the Lord this is true. The beautiful story of Joseph is the focus now for some eight chapters in Genesis. This portion of his life reads like a novel: from poverty, to prison, to palace! God's hand is clearly seen in all that transpires in our young hero's life.

Van

Let us look first at how GOD REACTS. No passive father here! He is obviously orchestrating events to bring about His ultimate will for Joseph.

We see Joseph in serious trouble! As I mentioned in the beginning of this sermon, he is sold as a slave and eventually lands in prison because of false charges. Briscoe writes, "By the time he had reached his early twenties Joseph had experienced enough discouragements to last most people a lifetime."[7]

However, "while Joseph was there in the prison, the Lord was with him; He showed him kindness and granted him favor in the eyes of the prison warden."[8] This, like many of the verses confirming the Lord's favor on Joseph, drives home the fact that God was actively engaged in Joseph's life.

There will be many times in the Christian's experience when we will be pushed around by the harsh realities of life. Some of these experiences may be severe, threatening to suck all the energy for living out of us! Make no mistake about it: life is beating lots of people to a pulp! You may be part of that painful reality.

Living with HIV status at times overwhelms me! The shock of realizing I will probably die young is hard to face. Knowing I have brought this on myself by my foolish and sinful choices makes it even worse.

However, God is the source of my strength! I could not make it a day if I didn't have Him in my heart. He gives me what I need to face each day at a time and make the most of what is ahead of me. I pray, naturally, that He will make it possible for me to live a long, somewhat normal life. If I don't, however, I know He will be my strength to face whatever is ahead of me!

He can be your source of daily strength also. Your situation may not be as critical as mine, or it may be worse. Let us pray, however, in the midst of the "prison" in which you find yourself, you can see how God is actively working behind the scenes to bring about what is good for you.

Charles

This week I was listening to a Christian radio talk show and heard the story of Rev. Bob Record. This man is the head of the North American Mission Board of the Southern Baptist Convention. When he was six months old, his mother died. His father was an alcoholic and drug addict. The dad abandoned Bob and his older sister.

(By the way, I want to honor the memory of my father by saying that he never abandoned his family. At least, he never walked out on us and left us to fend for ourselves. He had his personal problems and lived a miserable life until he was saved and changed by the power of the Holy Spirit, the church, and Christian friends. During those really bad years, however, he stayed with Mom and us! He never divorced her and kept his job to provide for our

family. At my stage of life, I have a perspective on his life and decisions that causes me to greatly honor his memory.)

Let's return to Bob Record's story. A wonderful family adopted Bob and his little sister. God used them to take up the slack that was obvious in these little kids' lives. Dr. Record became a Christian and wonderful minister of the gospel; God was operating in this little boy's life, wasn't He?

Van

God provides second, third, fourth, and many more opportunities for those of us who need them.

The second reality we look at in Joseph's experiences is GOD RECONCILES.

Eventually, according to the account in Genesis, an opportunity arose for Joseph to interpret Pharaoh's dreams. This led to the job he had when his brothers came to visit him, seeking food from the grain-rich Egyptians.

Thirteen years had passed when the brothers came to Egypt. Joseph is now a thirty-year-old man with heavy responsibilities on his shoulders. He is "governor over the land."[9] Food and shelter, culminating with a great family reunion, would be provided. It would also mark the beginning of God's people safely placed in the land of Goshen in northern Egypt where they would grow numerous and prosperous. It was the wonderful, providential hand of God at work.

However, there was the matter of the unfinished business between Joseph and his brothers. Remember, they had sold him into slavery. If it had not been for his brother Reuben, they might have killed him.[10] Things had to be put right between these boys, and God used Joseph to see that would happen!

Here is another important lesson: "unfinished business" in your or my life will never allow us to find complete peace until it is faced and resolved. There are people trying to get on with their lives only to find it hard to sleep, or deal with other anxieties, and it is all because of some situation we refuse to face and deal with it.

Joseph's plan was to allow the brothers to face their terrible deeds. His actions were a mixture of positive things, such as, "They drank and were merry"[11] and accusatory statements like, "Why have you repaid good with evil?"[12] He held one brother, Simeon, in prison at the end of the first visit[13], yet he replaced the money they used to buy the grain and gave them extra provisions for the return trip home.[14]

Here's the interesting thing: each event, good or bad, seemed to cause the brothers to think of past deeds. Time will not allow us to look in detail at how all of this was coming together, but a study of the scriptures will reveal the calculated plans and steps taken by our hero were designed to lead the brothers to face their actions of twenty-three years earlier!

It all came together when Joseph, still not recognized by his brothers on their second trip to Egypt, sets up a scheme to hold Benjamin as a prisoner. The governor agrees to let the men return home, but they will have to leave their youngest brother in Egypt. Here is their chance to gain freedom; all they had to do was to abandon Benjamin, grab their sacks and head home. After all, they had done this twice before when they abandoned Joseph in Dothan and then left Simeon as prisoner in Egypt at the end of their first trip.

Judah is now the hero; he steps forward and offers to stay in Egypt in the place of young Benjamin.[15] He demonstrates what is probably true of all the brothers—concern for the fate of their father if Benjamin is not allowed to return.

I always cry when I read the forty-fifth chapter of Genesis! The "family aspect" of Joseph, the Hebrew lad, overrides the role of the Egyptian Governor. As he weeps, Joseph has all the Egyptians to leave the room. He then reveals his true identity to his brothers. He gives the theological foundation for what has transpired across the years when he says to them, "God sent me ahead of you to preserve for you a remnant on earth and to save your lives by a great deliverance. *So then, it was not you who sent me here, but God.*"[16]

Obviously, a great deal of forgiveness is required for this great thing to happen. Thank the Lord that Joseph refused to hold a grudge against his brothers. The world would have given him permission to do so. He could have justified it in his mind, perhaps. However, he would not allow himself to do that.

Van

God reconciles! Some of the greatest stories throughout history are how family and friends, and even nations, have been reconciled after bitter separation.

Dads, do you need to be reconciled with an estranged child? Kids, what about you? Are there people at work, neighbors, or anyone against whom you hold a grudge? If so, consider reconciliation. Be a forgiver so you can move on! Living in the past does not move us forward with the plan God has for our lives.

The third reality we look at in Joseph's situation is GOD REWARDS.

Seventeen years later, Jacob died.[17] The brothers were afraid Joseph would now want to take revenge on them. They went to him, hoping to offset any plans he might have to hurt them.

Joseph's commitment earlier to "forgive and forget" was genuine. His reply to them, much like what he had said earlier, is another great passage from this outstanding story. He said, "You intended to harm me, but God intended it for good to accomplish what is now being done, the saving of many lives. So then, don't be afraid. I will provide for you and your children. And he reassured them and spoke kindly to them."[18]

God had rewarded not only Joseph for his faithfulness, but the entire household of Jacob was protected and blessed in many ways. Joseph was reaping the rewards of God that, in time, would spill over to the entire Hebrew nation!

I never dreamed that Dad and I would be here together, sharing our hearts with you on a Father's Day! At times, it has been uncomfortable. However, it is one of the great things in my life: to feel so close to Dad and to know that we are arm in arm, marching up the road in the same direction. That is a reward of great value to me.

Charles

I, too, am thanking God, Van, for the honor this is for me to share the pulpit with you. I pray it will happen every Father's Day for many years to come. *(Applause)*

How does God want to reward you? What is He calling you to do that will please Him and open His windows of blessings upon you?

I mentioned the alcohol problems my father had as a young man. However, the last thirty years of his life, he lived for God. He was active in the church and every Sunday visited the hospitals, giving out materials and praying with the sick. As I am proud of Van, so am I proud of my dad because I see the "before" and "after" touch of God on his life.

Malachi the prophet said, speaking for God, "I will send you Elijah, the prophet, and he will turn the hearts of the fathers to the children and the hearts of the children to their fathers."[19]

"Men Restoring the Walls"
(June 2001)

Van

This is the third year Dad and I have presented a message on Father's Day. The first time we preached a dialogue sermon, we did a message on The Prodigal Son. This is somewhat similar to our family situation where I had gone away from the Lord and I was welcomed home by my parents.

The second message we presented was about The Prodigal Parent. We talked about what parents might do to push kids away and make the "far lands" more attractive.

This year, we decided we would do things a little differently. We are going to look at the story of Nehemiah. If you do not know this man, well, you need to. You will be impressed with the many skills with which he was endowed and how he faithfully utilized those gifts in bringing about God's will at a very difficult time in the history of the Jews. <u>The Message of Nehemiah</u> relates how "Nehemiah, one of Israel's great leaders, tells firsthand the powerful story of the rebuilding of ancient Jerusalem's walls after the exile. This rebuilding, in the face of great odds, represented the people's renewal of faith, their overcoming of national shame, and the reforming of their conduct. He must surely be regarded as one of the most inventive and resilient personalities in the rich tapestry of Old Testament biography."[20]

The theme of our sermon is "Men Restoring The Walls." Obviously, it is Father's Day so we want the focus to be on the role men play in the family. As we look at the story of Nehemiah, keep in mind that he is going to represent men, particularly the role of leadership that is given to the man of the home. The *walls* being rebuilt stand for the problems or difficulties in the home that need attention. As we all know, family relationships can be easily broken down.

Let's read together Nehemiah 1:1-11 and 6:15-16.

1. The words of Nehemiah son of Hacalia: In the month of Kislev in the twentieth year, while I was in the citadel of Susa,

2. Hanani, one of my brothers, came from Judah with some other men, and I questioned them about the Jewish remnant that survived the exile, and also about Jerusalem.

3. They said to me, "Those who survived the exile and are back in the province are in great trouble and disgrace. The wall of Jerusalem is broken down, and its gates have been burned with fire."

4. When I heard these things, I sat down and wept. For some days I mourned and fasted and prayed before the God of heaven.

5. Then I said: "O Lord, God of heaven, the great and awesome God, who keeps his covenant of love with those who love him and obey his commands,

6. let your ear be attentive and your eyes open to hear the prayers your servant is praying before you day and night for your servants, the people of Israel. I confess the sins we Israelites, including myself and my father's house, have committed against you.

7. We have acted very wickedly toward you. We have not obeyed the commands, decrees and laws you gave your servant Moses.

8. "Remember the instruction you gave your servant Moses saying, 'If you are unfaithful, I will scatter you among the nations,

9. but if you return to me and obey my commands, then even if your exiled people are at the farthest horizon, I will gather them from there and bring them to the place I have chosen as a dwelling for my Name.'

10. They are your servants and your people, whom you redeemed by your great strength and your mighty hand.

11. Oh Lord, let your ear be attentive to the prayer of this your servant and to the prayer of your servants who delight in revering your name. Give your servant success today by granting him favor in the presence of this man." I was cupbearer to the king.

6: 15-16

15. So the wall was completed on the twenty-fifth of Elul, in fifty-two days.

16. When all our enemies heard about this, all the surrounding nations were afraid and lost their self-confidence, because they realized that this work had been done with the help of our God.

Thank you and please be seated.

Charles

Let me present a quick summary of what the story of Nehemiah is all about. It is a beautiful one that every man, father or grandfather, needs to read. It is important to be reminded God has called us to be the leader in our homes. Moreover, God intends for us to repair any wall that may have been broken down in our family.

It is probable that each of us could take time this morning to give testimony of a breach in the wall of our homes and families. We might talk about failing in our marriage, things that we have done (or should have done) that have had negative impact on our family.

Others of us might talk about ways we have let the wall be breached as it relates to our children. For instance, I have Van with me on the podium today not only because he is an excellent communicator, but he also is a reminder to me, and to this congregation, that there were times when the walls were down in Van's and my relationship. Let me assure you, I know I contributed tremendously to the falling apart of those walls! However, God is repairing the walls; He is building them up in our relationship and throughout our family. That is why we enjoy working together so much. Whether it is preaching, singing, or counseling together, it has been a wonderful journey for both of us. In addition to that, I am receiving so much help from him as more and more he becomes my counselor.

Back to the story of Nehemiah. In 587 B.C., the Babylonians destroyed Judah. They tore down the walls of Jerusalem, burned the homes of the people, and destroyed the glorious temple that Solomon had built. In the process, they carried away gold and priceless pieces of the temple, making a mockery of God.

As we look at all of this from God's perspective, we learn He had (actually) orchestrated it. Through His prophets He had already warned the people that their continual disobedience would result in severe punishment. Jeremiah had even pinpointed the seventy-year period of imprisonment by the Babylonians. The prophet of God had encouraged the people to not resist, but to settle down and make the most of it.[21]

A Voice From Heaven

This was the darkest period in the life of the Hebrew people, worse than when they were in Egyptian bondage.

Then, toward the end of the seventy years, some of the people began to return to Judah. They tried to reestablish themselves, but had little success. Leadership was weak. Moreover, the temple, the center of religious, political, and social life of the Hebrews, was not functional; it was still in disrepair. So under the leadership of Zerubbabel[22], some twenty years later, the temple was rebuilt. Though it was nothing like the glory of Solomon's temple, it was at least a means of some hope for the people.

Practically speaking, however, with the walls of the city down, there was no encouragement of any solid growth or development of the city. Can you imagine what it would be like if your house had no doors, windows, or other ways of keeping out varmints, bugs, and unwanted people? It would not be much of a home, would it? Neither was Jerusalem much of a city since it had no protection; it was vulnerable and just existed!

Nehemiah received word from his brother Hanani that the walls were down and the doors burned. God drove that information deep into the heart of our hero to convey he was to return to the city and rebuild the walls. God had not permanently cast off His people. The intention of our Creator was yet to unfold. Through His chosen people, the Messiah would come to offer hope of salvation from sin and eternal life to the entire world.

Van

There are four aspects to this story. Those are:

I. *Rebuilding Walls Begins with A Vision*
II. *Rebuilding Walls Depends on A Plan*
III. *Rebuilding Walls Evokes Opposition*
IV. *Rebuilding Walls Merits Celebration*

When Nehemiah's brother came to him with news of the walls being down, it is important to remember that this had been a fact for almost one hundred fifty years. It's true they did not have telephones, faxes, e-mail, or other modern day communication technology. Nonetheless, the information had surely filtered into the Persian court where Nehemiah served the King. Perhaps travelers who passed through the area left bits of information here and there. The point is, the situation in Jerusalem had been bad for a long time. So what is the importance of this fact? *The chosen people did not feel very "chosen" and, by and large, were unconcerned about Jerusalem.* Either that, or they felt there was absolutely nothing they could do about it, so they just accepted the fact and lived with it.

Not unlike many of us, is it? There is many a home where some "wall" is down. A bad marriage, trouble with the kids, emotional distance, or deep aching in the heart of a member and everyone just "looks the other way" and lives with it.

Just learning to live with a bad situation is very sad, and in many cases, it is unnecessary. I realize no family is perfect, nor will any ever be. However, there are many steps that can be taken to alleviate some of the heaviness you face in your home. For that to happen in most homes, however, there has to be a "wake-up" call.

Nehemiah's wake-up call was the message from his brother. Not the most recent news, but news that, this time, awakened his heart and mind in such a manner he was deeply touched and determined to do something about it.

Charles

Van wisely points out the insidious danger of becoming numb to hurting reality! One of the really painful realities of human life I have observed across the years is "manageable dysfunction" in a family. A family may be slowly bleeding to death, but everyone just muddles on as though everything is normal. That's not what God intends for our families.

As bad as that reality is, it's understandable. Today, as I did to Van some time ago, I confess I was as guilty as the next guy in just "looking the other way" at the wall that was torn down between him and me. It was a dark day in our family's life. However, God in His mercy sent us a "wake-up" call in the form of our son's bout with cancer. (More about that later; I'm getting a little ahead of the story.)

Rebuilding Walls Begins with A Vision

The Bible says when Nehemiah heard the news from his brother, he began to weep, fast, and pray. In that sad and painful time, however, God gave him a vision. There was reason to hope. Though the situation was deplorable, there were things he and God, working together, could get done. Before, he had just lived with the situation. Now, with the urging of God's Spirit, he was ready to make some changes.

I am sad to say there was a time when I also gave up on my son. I was angry with him for his choices and even angry with the Lord for what had happened in Van's life as a child. Things became so dark; there was even a time when I came close to just cutting him out of my life. It was not that I would refuse to see or talk with him. I just wanted to "give up" and not really expect things to get better.

But love would not let us go! Thank God, the deep love we had nurtured for each other across the years was more powerful than Satan's lies to us that we ought to just walk away from any kind of close father-son relationship. When "push came to shove" as it is said, love won out!

(By the way, Van could tell a similar story about being tempted to give up on a "hard-headed" father who was better at preaching at him then dialoguing with him.)

The vision the Lord gave to us was to not give up hope. Moreover, we were to take specific steps to set things right.

Our admonition to fathers or grandfathers is to ask God for a fresh vision of how walls torn down in your family can be rebuilt. Don't give up. It is important to cling to the dream you had at one time for your family. Regardless of how bad the situation may be in your marriage, your relationship to your kids, or whatever, keep holding on to the vision that God, working in and through you, is powerful enough to do something about it! That's the vision Nehemiah embraced and he is our example.

Harry Kemp says, "A poor man is not he who is without a cent (read: 'a perfect family'), but it is he who is without a dream, without hope."[23]

Van

We have mentioned before that there were times when Dad and I had given up on each other. I already knew this. But you know what, Dad? (*Looking at me*) It broke my heart again when I heard you say it. It's not a pretty thought, is it?

Still, I say, let's not give up on our family! Some of the greatest times we have had as father and son have been since we determined, under God and with His assistance, that we were going to mend the wall that had fallen down between us. Today, I can see my father in a different light. I listen not only to his words, but to his heart as well.

If you are an adult child with some kind of pain related to parents, and you feel that things are too late between you and them, let me encourage you to think differently. It may not be easy, and the ultimate outcome may not be perfect, but things can be improved if we just accept that kind of "vision-thinking."

If you are sitting here today thinking about how you have not spoken with your parents, or your kids, for some time, go home and do something about it. Talk person to person with them if possible. If not, write them. If they are deceased, you might even consider talking with someone about the situation and say something like, "If my dad (mom, child, etc.) were here, here is what I would say to them." Then proceed to tell what you would say if it were possible. It is amazing how that seemingly futile exercise can bring a sense of relief and closure to a bad memory!

Rebuilding Walls Depends on A Plan

Nehemiah developed a plan to go with the vision God gave him. In chapter one we see him awakened by the news from Jerusalem. His deep despair, however, led him to do something about it.

A Voice From Heaven

Incidentally, maybe the first step we must take in getting a vision and developing a plan is to be brokenhearted! Have you wept bitterly about the broken walls in your home? Have you fasted and prayed to God, confessing your sin as well as the sins of your fathers? Nehemiah is our model at this point.

In chapter two, Nehemiah is going to the king with a plan. In chapter one, we relate to him as a deeply *spiritual man*. Now, we see him as a very *practical man*. He used his position as cupbearer to the king to approach him with specific requests.

A cupbearer, by the way, was one who tasted food and drink before it was given to the king. He was a highly regarded and trusted servant of the nobility. The very life or death of a king or queen depended on the integrity of this person.

The job was a cushy one! It resulted in a certain level of prestige, financial well-being, and security for the future (as long as the king was alive, of course).

Give the man credit. He was ready to give this security up for the sake of his vision. True leaders with a passion to fulfill a vision are always people who sacrifice something or the other. What are you willing to sacrifice to mend the broken walls in your family?

Listen to Nehemiah: "I need permission to be gone for the time necessary to bring stability to Jerusalem. I will need timber to build the walls and letters from you to grant safe passage through certain countries" (the trip was eight hundred miles in length). The king gave Nehemiah all he had requested and included an entourage of soldiers for his protection.[24]

The plan included surveying the damage firsthand, and assessing what steps would be necessary to rebuild the wall.[25] It was easy for Nehemiah to see how important it was for everyone to have a part in the reconstruction.

There is design and direction in the plan Nehemiah had for the rebuilding. In addition to being a leader, the man was an able administrator. Note the unfolding of his plan:

1. There are seven names, locations, and responsibilities identified by Nehemiah.[2]

2. The builder's priority was the Sheep Gate and it was to be led by the priests.[27] What a dramatic way for Nehemiah to say, "Put God first," by repairing the portion of the wall that facilitated the sacrifices in worship. Note also that the priests were to work, setting an example for the people to follow!

3. Many of the families were assigned portions of the wall near their home. What motivation this would afford to work hard and to do a good job! After all, your own family would benefit if the wall was well-built and strong.[28]

Much more could be said about Nehemiah's plans to see the task accomplished. The overriding idea, however, is that he gave thought to *what* needed to be done and *how* to go about doing it.

We should not lose this lesson. With a vision, a strong desire to address the needs of your family, think through the necessary steps you will take to see the vision become reality. In Nehemiah's situation, as far as we know, he was strong enough to come up with the necessary plan on his own. You or I, however, may want to seek counsel from other family members, trusted friends, or even professional counselors.

Things don't have to perfect, of course. Do your best, even if you approach the task unsure that you have all the components in the right place. General George Patton said, "A good plan today is better than a perfect plan tomorrow."[29]

Charles

Son, there are two things we talked about that often destroy the vision a man has about helping his family. Share those with the congregation.

Van

You're right, Dad. There are two pitfalls to avoid in rebuilding your broken wall. One is *pride* and the other is *passivity.*

In Nehemiah's situation, there were some who allowed their pride to keep them from being part of the rebuilding.[30]

I can relate. Many of you know that I have shared my story of being sexually abused as a child and how that tremendously impacted my life in negative ways. Those years of growing up, I knew something was wrong. I was questioning and fearful. Most of all, I was ashamed to acknowledge I had the kind of homosexual thoughts that filled my mind. It was my pride that kept me from going to my parents. I kept assuring myself that, with time, everything would be okay, and life would go on for me in a normal way as I so desperately wanted it to do. To tell anyone about my struggles, however, was not an option open to me. People, maybe even my family, might reject me and I would be worse off than before. So I just hid behind my pride and said nothing.

Some of you may be keeping something inside you that needs to be dealt with, but your pride keeps you from opening up and dealing with it. If that is so, you must ask yourself, "Is maintaining my prideful status of greater value than rebuilding the wall torn down?" When you get right to the heart of things, what is more important to you?

The second pitfall to avoid in rebuilding your broken wall is *passivity*. As mentioned earlier, this was one of the main reasons nothing had been done before now. People had just adjusted to a less-than-ideal situation and tried to make the most of it. I imagine some of the people in Jerusalem, instead of looking for the main gate to enter when passing through, just took a "short-cut" and went through a hole in the wall.

Too many of us are guilty of taking a "short-cut" when it comes to addressing our broken wall situation. We get stuck in place and give in to despair.

Charles

Let me give an illustration fresh from Van's and my relationship.

Our grandson Neal visited with us this past week. Like his granddad, Neal loves to play golf. He came to spend the week with us in order to take part in a golf school out where we live. It was a golfer's paradise: lessons in the morning and then all the golf you wanted in the afternoon.

With the longer days during summer and the rearranging of my schedule to spend time with Neal, he and I played golf every day this week except two. On Friday, he and I played in a tournament to raise money for *Youth For Christ*. (We won first place, by the way!)

Anyway, yesterday after the wedding here at the church, Van and I were riding home together and were discussing this sermon we would be sharing with you this morning.

In the process, I felt strongly impressed to ask Van a question. Looking back now, I am confident it was the Holy Spirit urging us to deal with some of the very things we are presenting in this sermon. I asked him if he resented in any way the fact that I had spent so much time with Neal this week. I could tell it was a painful question. After a pause he replied, "No, I don't mind you spending so much time with him. But I know that you have probably thought on many occasions, 'I wish I had a son like this who loved to play golf with me.'"

Van

When we got home and pulled into the driveway, I wanted to go to my room and close the door. I just wanted to get away from him as I thought, "Oh boy, here we go again. I'm not measuring up; I'm not good enough for him!" Those were some old tapes playing in my mind, *but they were false tapes*. I kept thinking to myself, "I *am* good enough! He *does* love and value me!" If I had gone to my room and sulked in that moment, the lies would have taken on the form of reality. Instead, we discussed it at length sitting in the driveway. It was a very healthy experience for both of us to get a fresh view of the very things we would be sharing from our hearts with you today.

I don't need any other dad than the one God has given me. I have a great mom whom I love very much, but there are some things she can't do for me; things I need from my father. He is not going to abandon me and I am not going to give up on him. If the Lord allows it, we will preach Father Day sermons for years to come. (*Applause*)

Rebuilding Walls Evokes Opposition

Charles

Let's see. We've covered the first two ideas of successfully rebuilding walls: have a *vision* and have a *plan*. Now we come to the painful fact that, anytime we seek to make things right in the eyes of God or others, there will be opposition.

First, some of the non-Jewish residents in the area resented the effort to restore Jerusalem by providing secure walls. They mocked the efforts of Nehemiah and, when that did not work, they threatened violence against him. Then, coming up short in that effort as well, they tried to convene meetings with Nehemiah and the leadership to talk them out of the projects at hand. Everything they tried failed because Nehemiah responded with faith in God, encouragement to the people, and a plan to respond to each situation.[31]

The second form of opposition came from the Jews who had liked things the way they were in broken-down Jerusalem. Some of these fat cats were taking advantage of the poor of the area by charging them high interest rates.[32] As is often the case for the needy, this kept them in a financial hole and in a state of depression. Nehemiah called these loan sharks together and reprimanded them publicly. He exhorted them to do the right thing by their fellow countrymen and to return the confiscated farms, olive groves and repay the exorbitant fees they had collected.

Thankfully, these men agreed and it signaled a new day for everyone in the area!

For us, the lesson is clear. When we begin to mend the broken walls in family relations, we can be sure we'll run into disappointing situations that could derail our plans.

The Bible teaches us that Satan and the demons of hell are determined to halt any spiritual progress we might make.[33] A recurring theme of the Apostle Paul's is to be ready for spiritual battle with forces of evil.[34]

Van

I remember a time, Dad, when you and I had been working hard to mend some walls between us and we had a big "blowup." I was so discouraged, I wanted to give up.

Charles

Or strangle me.

Van

Either one would have worked well at the moment!

Rebuilding Walls Merits Celebration

For the sake of time, let me mention the last of the four elements in rebuilding walls. When we begin to see progress, small though it may seem, we must embrace with gratitude what good thing we see and celebrate it.

Nehemiah and the people of the area rebuilt the wall around Jerusalem in a record fifty-two days.[35] After that, they gathered to renew their vows to the Lord and to celebrate the mercies of God upon them. It was a time of great joy because first of all, it was a time for them to confess and repent of their sins, which had led to the breakdown in the wall to start.[36]

An unusual aspect of celebration from the Judeo-Christian perspective is that sadness and joy are often interrelated. Jesus said, "Blessed (happy) are those who mourn."[37] It is true that we may have to plow through a lot of sad and depressing stuff to get to the place of celebration. That is okay; it is a small price to pay.

Speaking for kids who have had a breakdown in relationship to their parents, let me assure you that we are not speaking of perfection. It does not exist this side of heaven. Dads, you don't have to be perfect just as the kids are not going to be perfect. Still, we can celebrate when things go well among us. Instead of looking at the things we don't have in our relationship, how about we celebrate the things that we do have in place?

We need to get excited about how well things are between us. After all, our fathers have been there for us, to guide and assist us. Can we celebrate? Can we be joyful and supportive of our fathers? Let's do it!! On the count of three, yell with me, "GO, DAD, GO!" *(The youth yell with Van.)* Let's do it again, louder, "GO, DAD, GO!" *(The young people are on their feet at this point, shouting at the top of their voices.)*

I love this man. Perfect? No. Neither am I. But we are working on it together; we are rebuilding the wall. With the help of the Lord, I will never give up on my dad again. I am prepared to work through whatever situation, good or bad, we may face for the rest of our lives.

What about you? Will you make that kind of commitment in your heart and to the Lord that, with His guidance and empowerment, you will also rebuild walls that have been pulled down in your family? God help us. *(Applause)*

Charles

Paul teaches us in Galatians not to get tired of doing what is right for we will eventually reap a harvest of blessing if we persevere.[38]

Before we leave, let me request of the ladies, youth, and children to remain seated. Would every married man in the building stand, please? *(They stand)* Those of you sitting down, would you pray for the men who are standing? One of them could be your husband, or your father. Pray for him and pray for the others.

Men, while our loved ones and friends are praying for us, let's remember how crucial we are in God's plan to bless and protect our family, to keep the walls strong. On this Father's Day, how many of you would say by lifting your hand, "I want to be the husband-father God expects me to be. I want to keep the walls of protection around my family. For those walls that are broken down, I pray God will assist me in embracing the vision to see them rebuilt. I need His strength and guidance in seeing they are restored. Pastor, pray for me." If this is your prayer, please lift your hand at this time.

As far as I can tell, that is almost 100 percent of the men standing who have raised their hand. Let us pray.

Father God, thank you for your countless blessings to us. Thank you for the fathers who stand and declare they want to be better husbands, fathers and leaders in their homes. Please give each of us the vision we need, the specific steps that are necessary, and the strength to overcome any opposition to making the walls of our homes strong.

We praise and thank you for all you do to enable us in the challenging walk we have.

In the name of Jesus, our Savior, we pray.

Amen

PART III

A VOICE FROM HEAVEN

FOREWORD

⁕

"Next to the idea of God, the idea of Heaven is the greatest idea that has ever entered into the heart of man, woman or child."[1] I agree. That hasn't always been true for me, I'm sorry to say. More often than I care to admit, my attention has been much more directed towards things of this earth than things of heaven. However, the death of Van and aging are changing this. My research on heaven is another major factor. The more I study and think about the eternal destiny of God's children, the more enamored I become with the subject!!

Randy Alcorn says, "Every human heart yearns for not only a person, but a place. The place we were made for. The place made for us. The place is heaven. The person is God."[2] Augustine said, "Oh God, thou hast made us for thyself and we are restless until we rest in Thee."[3]

I have heard there are statistics indicating that around 87% of American people believe in heaven.[4] Yet heaven is a "back-burner" issue to many, including some Christians. We believe in heaven; we just don't spend much time thinking about it or anticipating it. If the truth were known, I imagine that heaven is more a state of mind than it is a real place to a great number of people. It can mean all kinds of things to people. *"Heaven! The very word is synonymous with beauty, comfort, peace, satisfaction, and contentment. The adjectival form is often used to describe something wonderful, as in 'this roast is heavenly', or, 'the scenery is heavenly in New Zealand.'*

There's even a flavor of ice cream called, 'Heavenly Hash.'"[5] This is unfortunate. John Piper says, "When the heart no longer feels the truth of hell (or heaven), the gospel passes from 'good news' to 'just news.'"[6] Sadly, it often takes the passing of a loved one to awaken us to the hope of what God is preparing to give us beyond this life.

J. Oswald Sanders lists eight myths commonly held by those of us on this side of eternity.[7]

1. Heaven's main occupation will be sitting on a cloud, plucking the strings of a golden harp.
2. Everything is heaven will be bland, offering no challenge—nothing to look forward to with keen anticipation.
3. Heaven will consist largely of rest and contemplation, without absorbing occupation. ("To the activist on earth," Oswald comically asserts, " Perpetual rest would seem more like hell than heaven.")
4. Longing for heaven is weakness and a form of escapism. (Wisdom's note: The opposite is also a possibility. <u>Not</u> thinking about life after death is one way modern man sticks his head in the sand and pretends the afterlife does not exist nor merit much of his thought!)
5. There will be nothing interesting to do in heaven.
6. The music of heaven will be dull, heavy and repetitive.
7. Peter guards the pearly gates.
8. We become angels, wearing halos and wings.

No wonder we push the idea and hope of heaven to the edges of our daily lives. How tragic is this ignorance of the ultimate destiny of God's child! Heaven is so, so much more.

Returning to our contention that the idea of heaven is the second (after God) greatest idea man can grasp, it will be my goal in this section to present its reality and absorbing attraction in such a way that we will become homesick! Moreover, since my understanding of admittance to heaven is settled on this side of death, this book will be an appeal for any who read it and have not yet ventured to the cross to receive forgiveness and salvation.

"A Book Of Quotes"

When I was a Seminary student, one of my colleagues referred to a text we were using in a particular class as "a book of quotes." He was right; on every page of that book, there were almost as many quotes listed as there were original teachings or insights that came directly from our professor (who happened to be the author of that book). Then, we laughed and made light of the book. Now, I wish I had been kinder. In this treatise, I too am building on the insights and teachings of others who are more wise and insightful than I. Peter Kreeft in his <u>Everything You Ever Wanted to Know About Heaven</u> encourages freely using the wisdom of those who have gone before us. He speaks about "dwarfs standing on the shoulders of giants," and "Good philosophy is piggyback thinking: you stand on my shoulders, I stand on C.S. Lewis', Lewis stands on George MacDonald's, MacDonald stands on Augustine's, Augustine stands on the Apostle Paul's, and Paul stands on Christ's. That far up, you see far."[8] Thus, I gladly acknowledge my debt to the thinking of many people more insightful and creative than I in thinking about heaven.

Charles J Wisdom
September 2003

Author's Note

These "encounters" with Van you are about to read are not factual. Hearing Van's voice speak to me as recounted in the following chapters on heaven is a literary tool, a means of sharing some impressions I have about heaven. It also gives me a chance to think about what Van might be doing there and how it will be when we are there, as well.

CHAPTER 10 — A VOICE FROM HEAVEN

It was pitch-black in the bedroom when I awakened with a startle. I was experiencing another restless night—tossing, coughing, and not finding a comfortable position to sink into deep sleep. Squinting my eyes for better focus, I looked at the red lights on the clock by the bed and was surprised to see it was a little after 3:00 A.M.

Trying not to disturb Lilly Faye, I slipped out of bed and made my way to the kitchen for a glass of water. Sitting down to sip the water, my eyes fell on a portrait of Van over the fireplace. Almost automatically, I began to mumble prayers to God while at the same time talking to our recently deceased son. This is something I did almost every day; just earlier that evening I had walked outside, looked up into the moonlit sky and blurted out, "Son, we miss you so much. Please visit Mom or me in a dream or a vision. Oh God, let me see Van again."

Suddenly, it seemed as though the light over Van's picture grew brighter. I blinked, thinking I must still have sleep in my eyes. However, there was no doubt that a glowing light emanated from the face of Van. My first impulse was one of fear; I felt goose bumps run up and down my arms and legs. My heart began to race and the palms of my hands were instantly wet with sweat. I looked away in fear, then turned back to see that, indeed, there was a distinct difference about the portrait. Now I was terrified! I first thought maybe I was having some kind of a mental breakdown. "The grief is getting to me," I thought. I was surprised at how frightened I was becoming. My breathing was so loud I was certain it would awaken Lilly Faye who was sound asleep in the back part of the house. Oh Lord, what was happening to me?

To my utter amazement, as well as sense of relief, I suddenly began to feel at peace in my spirit. The light coming down from the portrait of Van had not disappeared. If anything, it was continuing to grow brighter. Nonetheless, the fear was rapidly leaving me and in its place were both serenity and a growing joy. Instead of looking away, I was now staring at the face of Van. Though the features themselves never changed, it seemed as though he was speaking to me. Now I was sure!! I heard his voice in my mind as he said, "Don't be afraid Dad. God has sent me to visit with you. It looks like we're going to be able to complete that book about our experiences as we wanted to do before I left earth." He paused briefly, then spoke with a tenderness that seemed to calm my nervousness.

"I know that you, Mom, Carla, Rose, and their families have grieved since I moved from earth to heaven. Your sadness is natural, and I have seen every tear each of you has shed. I really am there with you, as well as being with the many loved ones and friends I have had across the years. Sometimes when one of you laughs, I laugh with you. When you get excited about a particular event you are facing, I get excited too. You may not feel it, but I have wrapped each one of you in my arms and held you tightly on many occasions."

"However," he continued, "it's important to me that you, Mom, and the rest of the family fully accept my being in heaven instead of physically with you on earth. In coming weeks, I will share more with you concerning how wonderful things are in the presence of God. Though there has been a measure of healthy sorrow I was allowed to go through when I first arrived in heaven, the joy and sense of completeness in this place cannot be thoroughly explained, only experienced!"

For the first time, I spoke to Van. The atmosphere in the room was such that I, surprisingly, felt very comfortable in beginning this conversation with him. However, I also felt a tinge of confusion. "What do you mean, 'healthy sorrow'?" (That was just one of a hundred questions that were flooding my mind at the moment!) When he spoke of sorrow, I was surprised because I had always believed that when a Christian closes his eyes in death, he then opens them with complete perfection in every sense of the word. Such a state, I thought, would mean there would never be any kind of "healthy sorrow" in heaven.

In the first of many learning sessions for me, Van began to explain what had happened to him from the time he had taken his last breath. He told me that in that instant, he felt strong arms around him, ushering him upward in blazing speed toward the brightest light he had ever imagined. The "strong arms" statement made me think immediately of Lazarus in Jesus' parable who had been taken to heaven by angels.[1] It was as though the teaching about guardian angels watching over us[2] suddenly became a reality in my heart and not just in my mind. Even as I listened intently to what Van was saying to me, for I didn't want to miss a single word, I seemed to have this uncanny ability at the same time to ask myself, "Do I have an angel looking over my shoulder this very moment? Is he smiling at the sight of one who is at the same time sad and joyful, confused, yet being informed of important new insights?"

Now I found myself engaged at two levels: hearing every single word Van spoke to me, while at the same time my mind was spinning with related thoughts! Just being reminded that God's heavenly messengers and protectors were close by brought a sense of security.

I remembered how in 1956, the year I graduated from high school and entered college, five young missionaries to the Auca Indians of Ecuador were killed. Most of the Christian world knows the story of how many of these Native Ecuadorians were later converted and grew into strong Christians, some becoming ministers. In fact, their change was so complete that they no longer called themselves Auca, but changed their name to Wodani.[3] I heard one of these Indians, a spiritual leader among the Christians of his people, speak on a television program. He said, "We have gone from being 'head-hunters' to 'heart-hunters.'"[4] He also told of how the Indians who had killed the young missionaries saw white-robed beings above the tree line near the river where the killings took place. He said that, as Christians, they now believe these persons were angels, ready to escort the martyrs to heaven.

Back to the "healthy sorrow" statement. It sounded strange to me; I had never been exposed to the idea that perhaps there might be sorrow in heaven. Yet, I was aware that the Bible says, "God wipes the tears from their eyes."[5] For some reason, there is a time when we will cry in heaven. One person has explained these tears as "tears of joy" and referenced a sinful woman whom Jesus forgave.[6] "We are not told why she was weeping. It could have been due to her remorse over and repentance for sin or *to the joy over the forgiveness of her sins* [Italics mine]."[7] But why would God "wipe them from our eyes" if they represent joy? It seems to me He would welcome these tears.

C.S. Lewis suggests that the tears we have in heaven are because the deceased are themselves sorrowful at the time of parting and leaving loved ones behind.[8]

A pastor friend said he believes the tears in heaven are because the one recently arrived realizes there are family members or friends back on earth who are unbelieving or spiritually confused. They will not go to heaven when they die. Tears come because we are sad to realize we'll never be with them again. Or related, maybe we weep because we feel badly for not having prayed for or witnessed to these unsaved friends and loved ones.

That raises another concern: will heaven be heaven if we know a loved one is in hell and separated from God and us for all eternity? Won't Christian parents grieve at the realization a son, daughter, or grandchild is eternally lost? Pastor and author Erwin W. Lutzer makes this observation: "That question has so vexed the minds of theologians that some have actually asserted that in heaven God will blank out a part of our memory. The child will not know that his parents are lost in hell; the mother will not remember that she had a son."[9] There may be truth to that opinion.

I've never told anyone, including my kids, about a dream I had as a small boy. When I was converted to faith in Jesus Christ, my first concern was the spiritual wellbeing of my parents. Mom and Dad were not Christians. It is true they had attended a small Methodist church as children, but our family never went to church, prayed together, read the Bible in our home, or talked about the things of the Lord. As a new believer, I became concerned for their salvation. Dad had a serious drinking problem and he and Mom verbally fought a great amount of time. I prayed every day they would become followers of Jesus Christ.

One night, when I was around twelve years of age, I dreamed my dad died. In this dream, I was in heaven when it was "announced" that he had died and would spend eternity in hell. I remember vividly to this day the waves of sad emotions flowing through my body; I wept bitterly! Then, an angel gave me (strange, but true!) a bowl with strawberry ice cream in it. He said, "Eat this," and as soon as I tasted it, I was at perfect peace. I never told my family or anyone about this because it seemed so childish. I thought people would overlook the real impact of what that dream meant to me. I felt they would instead make light of my dream and the strawberry ice cream. Nevertheless, I found wonderful consolation in knowing that, somehow, God would make things right.

Van opened my understanding to a more complete perspective on the tears in heaven subject. "Initial sorrow in heaven," he said, "is part of the growth we will experience when we reach the celestial city."

"Growth" in heaven? What did that mean? I felt for a moment I was becoming more confused rather than more understanding about our eternal destiny. To repeat, my thoughts of what happens at death had always been that when we stepped from this life into the eternal dimension, we were in an instant made perfect; we would know all things just as we are already fully known by God.[10] What did he mean, "growth?"

"It works like this, Dad," Van said. "I've learned that when one passes from earth to heaven, he doesn't automatically gain instant omniscience. Truth is, Dad, we have an eternity to learn so much more than we can imagine about ourselves, about others, and about God."

"But heaven is a perfect place and we are all made perfect when we get there," I argued. Since I was a little child, I had always assumed anyone stepping across the portals of glory would immediately be one hundred percent like Christ, perfect and as informed as one could possibly be. Didn't the Apostle John teach, "When we see Him, we shall be like Him?"[11]

"The ultimate state of being is perfection and it does eventually come," Van replied. "The growth I have experienced in the months I have been here has been ten thousand times more impacting than the thirty-six years I lived on the earth. In fact, there is no way I could possibly compare the two. From that viewpoint, I think one could say that he is "perfect" compared to the way he was while on the earth. Nevertheless, heaven is at the same time both a place of perfection and a place of accelerated personal growth. And, believe me, my growth in understanding is just beginning!"

That really sounded interesting. I pressed for more information. Van's comments on heaven were whetting my appetite to learn as much as I could, as quickly as I could.

"In what ways do we grow in heaven?" I asked.

Van's explanations were insightful as well as mentally stimulating. It was of great interest to me to learn just how "human-like" we are in heaven. I was told that we look much the same in heaven as we do now on earth, except for the absence of disease or any negative results of a debilitating accident on earth. "Think about Jesus," he said. "After His death and resurrection, He looked basically the same to those who saw Him during the forty days He was on earth. True, there were some changes because of the nail marks in his hand and side.[12] However, He wasn't given His glorified body until He ascended to the throne to sit eternally at the right hand of God.[13] Even then, He is recognized by Stephen and identified as 'the Son of Man,' a title given Him on earth.[14] This strongly suggests a close tie between what He looked like on earth and what He looks like in heaven now."

I remembered my theology classes from seminary days. The well-respected theologian W.T. Conner asserts in his book, <u>The Gospel Of Redemption</u>, that there is growth in heaven. "It will be asked at once: 'Is not heaven a state of perfection, and does not perfection exclude the idea of growth? Heaven is a state of perfection. It is freedom from sin and its total curse. But a perfect state for man is not a state in which there is no growth. This is shown in the case of Jesus. He was sinless, but he grew. A state of perfection for a created being is rather a state in which everything that hinders growth is removed."[15] Later, in the same context, Dr. Conner writes, "Only God is omniscient. For a being who is not omniscient there is always room for growth."[16]

Van told me that in heaven our new personalities continue to grow. He said we don't become less human, but begin the process of being fully one hundred percent what God intended us to be all along! "Dad, it's almost like we are eternal children in heaven. Here, we're always eager to learn. There is a divinely-instilled curiosity in the citizens of heaven and we are hungry to understand more and more of the trillions of new truths God has for us."

"By the way," he continued, "that is just one of the reasons heaven is going to be anything but boring! Just think of having an insatiable desire to learn, to understand, and to have limitless opportunities with an eternity to search for more insight!! No barriers whatever to keep us from fully comprehending any and all subjects!!"

"We're like eternal children?" I asked. Before I could get the question out, it seemed Van spoke a verse to me in my spirit: "Unless you become like little children, you'll never enter the kingdom of heaven."[17] Wow! I remember preaching dozens of times across the years that the Lord calls us to the quick-to-believe faith and eager-to- learn spirit of small children! There, in His dominion, we will have endless ages in which to attain our possibilities.

Van continued. He told me that heaven is a place where, on entering, we begin to grow in at least three areas: in more fully understanding ourselves, in understanding others, and in understanding God. "The place I am starting, Dad, is getting an in-depth look at my experiences from childhood on. This, too, is a merciful and loving gift of God for those of us entering heaven." (He paused for what seemed to me a long time.)

"For instance, do you remember when the two of us went to see Christian counselor Michael Newman? I could tell you were really eager to get more information about why I had made some of the choices during those last couple of years at Baylor and the first three years after graduation. Well, here is good news: since I have arrived here, God is allowing me to see my past life *from a divine perspective* and with insight that is astounding! Dad, for the first time, I'm learning the answers to the many questions that have eaten at me since I was a small boy. Moreover, I am at the beginning of this wonderful and insightful learning curve. God is allowing me to see everything that has ever transpired in relation to me, good or evil, and He is thoroughly instructing me in the significance of each and every event!" All this he said with great enthusiasm in his voice.

"Could you be more specific?" I asked him. I was encouraged when he continued, "The good things that have happened to me from the time I was an infant are one by one passing before my eyes and I am literally reliving them. I feel the love, pride, care, and joy that you and Mom had every time you touched or even looked at me. I experience people smiling at me, speaking to me in loving and gentle ways. I feel a rush of care and protection not only from family members, but even people who cared for me when I was in the nursery at church. As I move through life, growing into toddler stage, these wonderful, loving experiences continue to repeat themselves. I knew on earth, like everyone does I suppose, that when I was a baby and totally dependent upon others, I was watched over by family, friends, even strangers. But now *I experience, I can feel* that wonderful security so freely given to me."

"You can *feel* them?" I asked. "So what you're talking about is more than just looking at a movie screen and being able to view your past?"

"You're right; it's incredible! As I said, it is something I cannot adequately explain. You have to experience it for yourself. It's as though I am reliving my life from birth, yet I am able to stand outside of myself to see it all occurring. The warm expressions of love, I not only see, but also am able to feel; I can actually enter into them."

What an amazing thing! My mind went back to the time when Van was very young. "Would you like for me to recall some of those times for you?" He seemed to know my answer and began.

"I have noted that when I was born in the middle of the night on October 6, 1965, you were so happy to have a son. I heard you saying to yourself, 'This is the first male Wisdom grandchild for Mom and Dad.' You could hardly wait for early morning to arrive so you could call Grandpa and Grandma Wisdom. I have heard your words to your mom when she answered the phone. 'Well mom, we have that grandson for you and Dad. Van Joseph was born just before midnight. He and Lilly Faye are doing great. I've already called the McKinneys and they are on their way up here to the hospital right now.' I heard the pride and joy in your voice, Dad."

He continued. "Do you remember when I was just a little over a year old and we were living in Wichita, Kansas? Mom had taken me to the barber for my first haircut, and the two of you agreed that afterwards she would bring me by your office at the church for you to see me. You looked out your office window and saw Mom and me walking up the church sidewalk. Dad, in my watching that event, I *experienced* the joy you had in seeing me. *Entering into that experience was such a rich gift to me!!*" He continued, "I was barely able to walk and had to hold on to Mom's hand. I saw the happiness in your eyes as you noted the little football shirt I was wearing with the name WISDOM on the back."

As Van described in vivid details those accounts, I began to weep. It was not only because I was getting to relive those experiences myself, it was because I was receiving assurances from Van that he knew he was cherished; that I was proud to have him as my son. I remembered a time when Van was around twenty-five, and we were arguing about his homosexual friends and choices. Things got pretty heated between us, and Van asked me straight on, "One question I have for you: are you even a little proud that I am your son? Or do you find yourself wishing I had never been born to you?" The pain in his voice sent me a clear message: *you do not love me or even care that I was born.* While I had known that things were being exaggerated in our heated discussion, I had thought of his question many times and wondered how it was possible that I could be sending that kind of message to him. I assured him I loved him and was pleased with many things about him. Still, both of us had left that scene deeply hurt.

Now, it was as though Van was giving me reassurances that God was allowing him to relive his life in such a way that he had no room for doubt. He knew he was loved and wanted. Praise God!! The peace this produced in my soul reverberated deeply inside!!

Then, in a split second, I didn't hear his voice anymore.

Now, I was in a state of ecstasy! I wanted to shout. I wanted to run to the bedroom and yell for my wife of forty-four years to come with me to the kitchen! However, I was unable to leave the spot where I was sitting. I couldn't take my eyes off the glowing portrait. My mind was filled with memories. Pictures of Van as a baby in Lufkin, Texas, and as a little boy in Wichita, Kansas seemed to speed through my head. It was like looking at a movie while holding down the fast-forward button. I saw him grow up before my eyes! There he was in Guadalajara, Mexico, and in Mexico City attending the American school. Scene after scene flew by and I saw him in middle and high school in San Antonio, Texas. Wow!! In one way, I was becoming dizzy with the fast-moving events. At the same time, these episodes were occurring in slow motion. It was mind-boggling to say the least. How was it possible that I was seeing so many years of Van's life at the same time both rapidly and slowly?

You can imagine the shock I felt when, as things seemed to return to normal, I glanced at the clock on the microwave and it was 6:25 A.M. What had seemed to occur in a brief period of time had actually taken over three hours to accomplish! Noting that the picture of Van was not glowing, I knew that this "visitation" was over. Yet I also sensed that it would not be the last time. Another voice inside of me was saying that there would be more extraordinary encounters with my son. I continued crying for several minutes, and then fell on my knees beside the couch to thank God for what He was allowing to happen.

CHAPTER 11 — TIME AND ETERNITY

Van's second visit with me gave me great insight into what he was enjoying in heaven.

"Dad, pull over to that mall. I want to talk with you." In place of the music I had been listening to, the familiar voice of my deceased son came through the radio, loud and clear. I guess it was a guardian angel that protected me from having a wreck, because my body, as when I visited with Van the first time, began to shake. Strange, isn't it? I immediately thought of the days when I was training as a pastoral counselor and interning at the Texas Research Institute of Mental Sciences (T.R.I.M.S.) at the Medical Center in Houston. One of the things we learned about people out of touch with reality is that they sometime hear voices speaking to them, often through their radio or television. In fact, I had led small groups of patients who told me of hearing people speak directly to them through their radio. One young gentleman even walked into the lobby of a large bank in downtown Houston and announced to the bank tellers that God had called his name on the radio, and told him to go to that bank and inform them they were to give him a million dollars!

That was the first thought that popped into my mind as I instantly pulled over in traffic to enter the parking lot of a large shopping mall. The sensation of fear and a pounding heart came over me as I stopped the car under one of the few trees in the parking area.

"Relax, Dad," Van said. So I did. Now, serenity filled me and I was excited with anticipation of what was about to happen. It had been two weeks since my encounter with Van in the early morning hours at home. To say I thought about that event every waking hour (and some sleeping ones as well) would be an understatement! I wondered when and how Van would show up again. When he did, I would have questions for him!! I was ready to unload on him:

... "What is heaven like?"

... "Have you spent time with the Lord? What about many of the Saints of the Bible? Have you seen or talked with them?"

... "What is it like being reunited with your grandparents, your Uncle Bill, Aunt Cora, and others?"

... "What age are you? Are you a child, the age you were when you died, or is there a uniform age everyone takes on when they enter heaven?"

... "Can you fly?" (I felt silly asking that one, but it is something I have wanted to know ever since I was little, and the child in me would just have to find out!)

... "What is a day like in heaven?"

... "Are you ever sad when you think about us here on earth who struggle with grief over your death?"

There were some other, even sillier, questions, which went through my mind those two weeks between our visits ("Seen any golf courses there?") Van must have anticipated my countless questions, so when I began to hear his voice again he said, "Dad, I will try to describe in ways you can grasp the magnificence of God, the people here, and the place itself. My explanations will fall short; the full impact of what God has prepared for His people can only be experienced. Descriptions are inadequate."

He continued, "Remember that statement on heaven you read in John Piper's book, 'Symbols of heaven in the Bible are understatements of reality'?[1] The realities of heaven cannot be grasped because of the limitations of human understanding. So, I'll answer you in ways that you can comprehend." (In that moment I experienced a tinge of parenting, of saying to my children when they were small, "I'm going to explain this in such a way that you can understand it." Truth is, I felt like a child during these mystical encounters!)

"It may help for me to begin answering some of your questions with an explanation concerning the issue of **time** in heaven. On one hand, time is much like it is on earth, with the exception of no need of night for rest.[2] However—hold on, Dad, because this will blow your socks off—there is no time in heaven as we understand it on earth. Therefore, <u>we are all together, at this moment, in heaven!!</u>

I was shocked! What could he possibly mean? His mother and I were with him? Carla and her family? Rose and her family? All of our deceased and living loved ones are already together? I thought that is what I heard him say. But that didn't make sense! We are on earth; he is in heaven. How can he mean we are at this present moment all together in heaven? My head was spinning.

"I don't understand what you are saying, Van."

"Dad, with God there is no sense of time the way it is accounted for on earth. In heaven, we are in a different dimension. As the scriptures teach, 'With God, one day is as a thousand years, a thousand years as a day.'"[3] Van also quoted the Almighty's words to Moses: I AM WHO I AM.[4]

When Van referred to that passage, it immediately brought to my mind the encounter Jesus had with some of the Pharisees of his day. He was bold in telling them Abraham, their "founding" father, had anticipated his (Jesus') coming to this world.

Our Lord was seeking to open their eyes to his true nature, viz. that He is the eternal God. I AM WHO I AM already existed before Abraham was ever born. Unfortunately, as is true of spiritually blind people, the Pharisees could not (or would not) embrace the concept that Jesus was claiming that He had always been in existence!"[5]

That part of what my son was saying I could understand. However, I was still fuzzy with the idea that all of my family, loved ones, friends, and all God's people *were at this present moment, already in heaven!*

Van explained more concerning the concept of time. The material world, our world of humans, knows only linear time; everything has a starting place and a straight line moving toward an ending place. In God's economy of time, however, in the eternal dimension, the situation is different! "In heaven, you, Mom, the girls and their families, and all of God's children are already there, together." I was trying hard to grasp what he was saying. I sat there with a blank look. He continued to explain that in heaven, though the Bible speaks of day, night, and time (so humans can understand), *eternity* is the operative word. Eternity envelops time; time is past, present, or future. Eternity is all three simultaneously. While this might seem impossible to us from our perspective of time, he reminded me, "With God, all things are possible."[6]

Noting my interest perk up even more, Van plunged deeper. "Strange though it may sound to you, we are all together in heaven." He quoted author Peter Kreeft. "A consequence of all time being present in eternity is that all lifetimes meet there, as different roads up the same mountain meet at the top. In death, we shall not only meet in the same place, but at the same 'time.' We will meet our descendants as well as our ancestors, and when we meet Abraham, he will not have been waiting for four thousand years."[7] He continued, "Professor Kreeft wrote, 'We are in heaven already, whether we know it or not, just as a fetus is already in the world, though the womb masks it from our eyes.'"[8]

"By the way, Dad, let me tell you an interesting story about Peter Kreeft; it will give you additional insight into this 'time and eternity' issue as it relates to God. When his daughter was diagnosed as having a fatal, malignant brain tumor, he asked his friends to pray for her. The prayers were effective because the tumor turned out to be benign. A skeptical friend of the family, who said he had nonetheless joined in praying for the girl, said to Dr. Kreeft, 'You realize, of course, that our prayers couldn't have changed anything, really; the doctor said the tumor had been in her for years and was benign from the beginning.' Dr. Kreeft replied, 'Your prayers <u>did</u> change things. God, <u>eternally foreseeing all those prayers, decided to give her a benign tumor instead of a malignant one when He created her</u> [emphasis mine].'" [9]

I was stunned yet again! I just sat there mulling over the impact of what I had just heard. The idea of praying for something in the near or distant future was familiar. I have been praying for years that God would give four hundred years of exceptional blessings to my kids, grandchildren, great-grandchildren, great-great-grandchildren, etc. *But I have never prayed for people and situations that were in the past!* This new insight helped me see, from God's time-perspective, one can pray today and have an impact on those things that have already occurred. Astounding!

There was a long period of silence when I heard Van's voice again.

"What do you think?" he asked. I may have had a hard time grasping at first what he was teaching me about heaven, but it began to make sense to me.

"Exciting thoughts," I replied. "However, I'm surprised to learn these things in part because I can't recall any teaching in the scriptures on this subject. I know, of course, that Albert Einstein's teachings on space and time emphasize earthly time being one dimensional, moving from beginning to ending. Space (eternity) is different."

"If you think about it, Dad, there are some scriptural hints of this concept of eternity having already started."

"Like what?" I asked.

"Like the teachings concerning the nature of God, for instance. The Bible reveals God from the very beginning as eternal.[10] Thus, He sees the future as clearly as the past. It is not because He must wait for things to happen; for Him they have already happened."

Van continued, "There is sequence of experience here in heaven, but it's not based on chronology. It has to do with spiritual readiness."

"What do you mean, 'spiritual readiness'?"

"I've mentioned that in heaven we continue to grow. Not everything is revealed to us at once. God has His ways of allowing things to unfold in the experiences of the citizens of heaven. When we are at the level that indicates we are ready for the next new insight or special encounter, additional understanding and growth takes place."

There was a pause as I processed this new information. It was a little fuzzy to me, but I could at least partially understand what he was saying. I remember having heard that in heaven we will know others and ourselves well in time, but we'll never completely grasp the nature of God. I guess we will be learners for all eternity in that way!

"Back to the subject of scriptural hints concerning the nature of eternity. In Revelation 13:8, reference is made to the crucifixion of

A Voice From Heaven

Jesus. We read, 'the Lamb, slain from the foundation of the world.' The cross occurred at a moment in history. The date is precise. Yet the Bible says it happened before the creation of the world."

He continued. "In Ephesians 1:4, we read again about something happening 'before the foundation of the world.' It concerns our salvation. Paul says we were 'chosen in Christ' even before the world was created. When you see eternity not as a succession of events in chronological sequence, but as relating to us in an entirely different dimension, you begin to more fully understand this concept."

"Let me share one other scriptural passage that sheds light on the subject of eternity being present *now*. Hebrews 11:40b refers to the saints of the Old Testament and makes this interesting statement: 'apart from us, they shall not be made perfect'."

I must have had a puzzled look on my face, because Van said, "A more modern translation of that entire verse says, 'Not one of these people, even though their lives were exemplary, got their hands on what was promised. God had a better plan for us: that their faith and our faith would come together to make one completed whole, their lives of faith not complete apart from ours.'[11] That means that all of God's people enter into the experience of perfection at once. It is not in sequence, not separated by chronology, but all at once."

"What you say makes lots of sense. I guess I just never thought of it in the way you explain. Still..."

He interrupted me, determined to make things clear.

"Dad, here is what I am saying: When a believer in Jesus Christ dies, he at once experiences the coming of Christ for His church. The believer steps out of time into eternity and the next event for him is the culmination of *time as it is experienced on the earth*. What is more amazing in my experience as a believer, *I have not left any of you behind!!* All of my Christian loved ones are here. Those of you who stood beside my grave and wept, then went home to a barren and gray house are with me, this very moment, in glory. You know what else? Since there is no time in eternity, I discovered that, to my amazement, just as I reached heaven, so did Adam."

"Son, what about the passage in Revelation 6:10-11 that says believers who were killed because of their faith will cry out to God, 'How long, Strong God, Holy and True? How long before you step

A Voice From Heaven

in and avenge our murders?' Then, each martyr was given a white robe and told to sit back and wait until the full number of martyrs was filled from among their servant companions and friends in the faith.' This seems to indicate there is a sense of time in heaven."[12]

Van replied, "Don't let me confuse you, Dad, but the martyred souls in this passage are identifying with the conditions on earth. They are in eternity, yes. However, on earth there is always the awareness of time, of delay, and of waiting. Since John is still on earth at the time of this writing, their concerns needed to be voiced in the language of time."[13]

"It's like this, Dad. Envision railroad tracks; they run side by side in the same direction. One of these tracks is marked 'eternity' while the other is marked 'time.' In heaven, those who step out of *time* (that is, those who have died) and moved into *eternity* (they are in heaven) have the ability to step back into *time* again for special occasions. Thus heaven's inhabitants are able to 'time travel'."

That grabbed my attention. "You mean we will be able to visit the past or the future at will?"

"Yes. Moreover, God uses this travel back and forth as one of the many interesting ways of giving us insight and experiencing the growth I told you about earlier."

Out of curiosity, I pressed for more detail. Was it a kind of "time machine" we would utilize in going from one era or year to another?

"No, not at all. Actually, Dad, you are already able to do this in a fashion," Van replied.

"What do you mean?"

"Well, just think about it. We were all created with the ability to 'travel' wherever we want in our minds. While on earth we are limited to just one physical place, but our mind can go wherever our imagination wants to take it. We can travel to the past or the future as we imagine it might be. We have memories that are so vivid, at times it seems we are reliving something that occurred years ago. In fact, as you know, things from our past can be so real and powerful, there are people on earth whose daily behavior is greatly controlled by their memories."

A Voice From Heaven

Silence. We were on the same wavelength at that moment. I thought about Van's experiences as a small boy being sexually abused and how controlling those devastating memories were to him in his early adult years. I remembered an occasion when Van and I were in a restaurant in Houston for lunch. He was seeing a Christian counselor and dealing with his childhood memories. When he met me at our table, he was so down in spirit! I sensed his emotional heaviness and in the beginning, few words were spoken between us. When we did begin to talk, he started mumbling, "How could anyone do something like that to a little child?"

I felt so helpless; all I could do was listen as he sobbed over and over, "Why? Why?" His eyes overflowed with tears as he cried louder and louder. Glancing around, I noticed several people looking our way. But I didn't care; my heart was broken for my son who, in his mind, *was reliving the tragedies of his childhood in that moment.*

"But Dad," he began, his voice communicating a spirit of contentment, "here in heaven the Lord makes it possible for people like me to find 'closure' to those unhappy, earthly experiences. That's just *one* of a countless number of good things awaiting those who are destined for heaven. As a matter of fact, God places that hope in the hearts of his children, causing them to long for eternal life and peace in His presence. You know, He doesn't want you to get too tied to this world and forget your 'temporary' status as an earthling."

I began to feel more uplifted in that moment. In fact, I was glad to understand more clearly: imaginative capabilities of our minds here on earth will become realities in heaven. After all, our minds serve us also by helping us to remember good things or *imagining* good things in the face of harsh reality.

For instance, Duane and Iris Blue are good friends to Lilly Faye and me. Before Iris found new life in Christ, she had a horrible early life. At a very young age, Iris became involved in alcohol, drugs, and prostitution.

She became a thief as well, robbing in order to have money to support her drug needs. However, she was arrested and spent time in prison where her belligerent attitude kept her in some kind of on-going trouble. Her testimony is that she spent many days in solitary confinement for bad behavior. However, she actually looked forward to those times when she was alone, because those were hours spent envisioning her "ideal life." For Iris, that perfect life was being a small, trim woman of culture. Iris had been a physically big person all her life. She was not obese, but big with large features. She had hated herself from the time she was old enough to know she was bigger than the biggest boys in school (and they would remind her of that)! She had been an outsider to most "decent" folk and coped with it by being even more antisocial in her behavior. But in her deepest fantasies, she was small in size and loved by others. She said on many occasions in the prison" hole," she fantasized that someone, through magical surgery, would cut her open and a small, beautiful, winsome woman would step out.

When Iris came out of prison, she went to work in a topless nightclub in Houston. However, through the goodness of God and His divine ways, a deeply committed Christian man met her and began to talk with Iris about her need of letting God love her and forgive her of her sin. She strongly resisted though she worked hard at keeping this young man as a friend; he was an encouraging testimony to her that not all men were out to get from her what they could. He persisted. One night, in the nightclub she was managing, according to Iris, "with music blaring so loudly you could hardly hear yourself think, he began to press upon me the need to pray and ask Jesus Christ to enter my life and change me. I had been thinking about what he had told me. It was making sense. Moreover, there was in me a restless discontent I could not comprehend. Now, however, I understand that I was under the influence of the Holy Spirit; He was tugging at my heart. I was a little surprised when I heard myself say to him, 'OK; I'm ready.' He told me that if I were serious, I would kneel down with him in the middle of that nightclub floor and pray with him to ask Jesus to come into my heart. Now, I was eager! I got on my knees and begin to pray in a loud voice, crying and praying at the same time." I've heard Iris tell this story of her conversion at least twenty times over the last several years. Her closing words always bring tears to my eyes: "I knelt down a tramp.... and stood up a lady!"[14]

My point in telling this true story is to point out how Iris used her imagination to escape the deep frustrations and realities of her life. That is what Van was saying; we are able to actually *experience* what we can only imagine here on earth!

I have said on several occasions that I hope in heaven we will be able to travel through history to see our lives as small children, students in school or college, or whatever. In heaven, I will want to go with Paul on one of his missionary journeys, or visit some important event in history several centuries ago. Wouldn't it be exciting to see young David fight the giant Goliath?[15] Or the crossing of the Red Sea?[16] I want to go back to New Testament days to watch the Lord Jesus perform miracles and teach powerful, eternal truths! One can only imagine what it would like to stand at the foot of the cross as Jesus atones for the sin of the world! Or to be at the tomb when He walked out of it.[17]

I've often thought of my dad as a youngster growing up in the swamps of south Louisiana. He lived in those old houses that had no electricity or running water. I've never forgotten the exciting account he shared with me on several occasions of how a boat he and five young people were riding in caught fire and sank. Mom told me that Dad was a hero in saving the lives of some of the younger kids until a nearby boat could rescue them. I'd like to see that and many other events in the early lives of my parents and grandparents. "After all," Van's voice summoned me back, "God is the creator of heaven and eternity. As creator, He is like the author of a book who can start at the end, go to the beginning, step outside of time and develop the story as He wishes. God has created heaven and eternity in the same way."

I thought of Elizabeth Sherrill's comments about the uniqueness of time in heaven. "Beloved figures like (C.S.) Lewis and (Henri) Nouwen, of course, will have millions waiting to meet them. If heaven ran by an earthly clock, there'd be long lines stretching from their doorways. But heaven's 'time', I suspect, is very different from ours…not only endless, but simultaneous. 'Yes, I'm free to see you right now,' Lewis will say to me and to all the others…and meanwhile be able to close his door and savor his cherished solitude."[18]

Just about the time I thought I was beginning to have a little insight into the issue of time in heaven, Van moved on in his discourse. "Moreover," he continued, "even from your perspective, you need to know that your earthly time is very, very short. You feel as though some days or weeks drag by slowly. Honestly though, Dad, don't you say to yourself or talk with others about how time seems to just fly? I listen to your conversations from time to time. Just a short while ago, I saw you and a pastor friend talking in the parking lot at Falcon Point Golf Club about the brevity of life. You had an animated conversation for fifteen or twenty minutes of how it was just 'yesterday' you were in grade school. Or how quickly your children grew up and left home. I overheard you tell him that the forty-four years of being a pastor seemed to be more like forty-four weeks."

That made sense. I agreed with Van; life really does move on quickly. When I was a child, it seemed a long time from one Christmas to the next. As an older adult now, however, Christmas seems to roll around every few months! The older I get, the faster times speeds by.

"Dad," Van called me back to his observations, "a person on earth may have a hard time capturing the idea of all times emerging in eternity. But you can understand the brevity of time. Elderly people will tell you that their life has been brief." I remembered that same emphasis given by C.S. Lewis in <u>Out Of The Silent Planet</u>,[19] and Peter Kreeft developing this thought in some of his writings. "There is (an interesting) phenomenon in world-history, world-time: it, too, speeds up, its time moves faster as the world ages. *More happens in less time with each era in human history.* (Emphasis mine) Why? Because we learn to live in larger bites, much as a maturing reader learns to read larger and larger groups of words. This is our way of unconsciously beginning to prepare for eternity, where the 'bite' is total, where we are present to all time at once."[20]

"What's so important about that? Just this: where it takes, perhaps ten or fifteen minutes now to think through a particular situation, we will be able to comprehend ten million such situations and do it in what would be a split-second on the earth! That means we will be able to sit down and have century-long conversations with loved ones, great men and women of history or of the Bible, or even with each and every individual who has ever lived on the earth and is with us in heaven. Time will be a non-issue in heaven!

A Voice From Heaven

Someone has surmised there may be billions of angels in God's creation. If time is not an issue, we will be able to know every one.

The idea that our family, plus all our loved ones and friends who are believers, are in Heaven *at this very moment* overwhelmed me! Van was not sad for us; we are all together from his perspective. Though we may miss him greatly, limited to this earth's domain, there was a sense of peace that filled my heart! Even now, when I am sad or lonely, I remind myself to look at things from heaven's viewpoint.

When my attention returned to Van, his presence was less pronounced. I knew he was "leaving" again. Like a distant voice, I heard him saying, *"I'll talk with you later..."*

I sat in the car on that parking lot for a long time, thinking. Van's insights into heaven made sense, but I had a hard time wrapping my mind around them. I reached for my Bible and turned immediately to the book of Revelation. I read rapidly, with each word seeming to literally jump off the pages; my appetite to know more was insatiable! I read:

.... the place itself is beautiful beyond description

.... the environment is one of perfect serenity and security.

.... the inhabitants of heaven are free from the curses of sinful life: no sickness, no tears, no fears, and no separation from loved ones.

.... the King of Kings, our eternal GOD, is the center of heaven and everyone one is eager to express love, adoration and worship.[21]

Heaven really is about God. Our fascination with streets of gold, beautiful jeweled walls, and other interesting teachings about our eternal home all fade away when one fully comprehends the centrality of God and eternity. I love the words of the chorus we sing at church, "I'm coming back to the heart of worship, and it's all about you, it's all about you, Jesus."[22]

Randy Alcorn writes about seeing the Lord Jesus Christ for the first time in heaven. In his novel <u>Deadline</u>, the character Finney enters heaven and meets his savior face to face.

"At the back of the crowd stood one Being flowing with a soft light that did not blind, but attracted and captivated the eyes. He smiled at Finney, who trembled with joy at the immediate realization of who it was.

This was the ageless one, the Ancient of Days, who is eternally young. He stepped forward...He who had spun the galaxies into being with a single snap of his finger, he who could uncreate all that existed with no more than a thought, extended his hand to Finney, as if the hand he extended was that of a plain ordinary carpenter.... For the moment, it was impossible to look elsewhere, and no one in his right mind would have wanted to.

'Welcome, my son! Enter the kingdom prepared for you, by virtue of a work done by another, a work you could not do. Here you shall receive reward for those works you did in my name, works you were created to do.'

And then, with a smile that communicated more than any smile Finney had ever seen, the Great One looked into his eyes and said with obvious pride, 'Well done, my good and faithful servant. Enter into the joy of your Lord!'

As the crowd broke out in cheers, Finney felt overwhelmed and dropped to his knees, then flat on the ground, face down, as if the knees were still too lofty a position before the Lord of Heaven."[23]

"Are there golf courses in heaven?" I had thought about this earlier when Van had first begun to speak to me at the mall parking lot. Now that I was driving toward our home, I was rethinking all the things that I had heard him say earlier. But my curiosity just got the best of me and I returned to the golf question. Having had a love affair with golf for thirty years, I wondered about this from time to time. I remember hearing someone say that golf in heaven would be boring because every shot would be a "hole in one;" no one lost or won because every golfer would be a perfect performer. However, Van had explained things differently. In heaven, when golfers tee it up, we will find ourselves reverting to our earthly skills status. Therefore, the challenge will be real. (The courses, naturally, will be beautiful beyond description!)

As I thought about it, I realized also that the competition would not be against the person with whom we are playing, but against the course itself. After all, isn't that the greatest attitude to take to the golf course? In the best spirit of competition, the golfer is not trying to beat his playing partners as much as he is being pitted against the challenges of the course! I am aware, of course, that many rounds of golf are played with the desire to surpass your companions. Unfortunately, some are motivated to improve their games so they will feel superior to other people. (Lord knows I have struggled with that demon in my own life on many occasions.) But no golfer will feel *inferior* or *superior* in heaven. Our stimulation will be in continuing to grow in our ability to overcome the course's obstacles.

And, thank the Lord, there will be no sore backs in heaven!!

FOREWORD TO CHAPTER 12

Once again I am "walking on thin ice" as I venture into arenas of heavenly details about which the Bible gives no answers. I tremble a bit when I think about how far from fact these "answers" may really be. I am being foolish if I give the impression I know the answers to these questions; I don't. After all, Paul reminds us that "eye hath not seen, nor ear heard, neither have entered into the heart of man, the things which God hath prepared for those who love Him."[1] I can no more describe heaven in detail than I could describe what earth is like to an unborn child in a mother's womb.

Nevertheless, I want to guess. I want to think out loud about questions that others and I have about our eternal home. If the reader will give me a little "literary license," I will offer some opinions about these questions.

The reader is free to disagree with me (as if you need my permission!!). If we discussed the information I present in this chapter and you called my hand on some of them, I would be non-defensive about it.

Having admitted my uncertainties, at least for the time, I will stand by them until I have better information from some other, wiser source. That, however, may not come until we get to the perfect home the Lord is preparing for His children.

Charles J. Wisdom

CHAPTER 12—QUESTIONS AND ANSWERS

Van, I have so many questions about heaven. Some of these are my own while others are questions people have asked over the years I have been a pastor.

Okay. And?

Well, let me throw out several of them in rapid fashion and you tell me what you know about the subject. After all, you have a front row seat.

Sounds good to me, Dad. Let's give it a try.

For one, where is heaven?

To start with, let's be reminded that heaven, the place, is in a different dimension from earth. Earth is physical, material. Heaven is "outside" of that in the sense that it is a "spiritual dimension."

But it *is* a definite place, isn't it?

It's *definitely* a real, specific place. Remember the words of Jesus to His disciples just before His crucifixion? Speaking of His pending departure, He said, "I am going to prepare a *place* for you, and I will come back and receive you to myself."[1]

Let's get back to your question as to where heaven is. It's not uncommon for people to think of heaven being located in "the heavens;" that is, up in the sky. One person said he thought heaven would be located beyond where space ends.

As you know, Dad, the Bible speaks of three heavens. There is the *created order*, which includes the earth, universe, and the solar system. Then, we are told of the *spiritual heaven*, which Jesus referred to when talking with Nicodemus.[2] This is a spiritual domain where God's angels and Satan's evil spirits are at work. Lastly, the *third heaven* is the heaven of your question. It is the place where God dwells. This is the heaven that is the final abode of the family of God. It is, as I said, in a different dimension from the other two mentioned.[3]

Speaking of heaven as being in a non-material dimension, I remember when the first Russian Cosmonaut walked in space. His name was Yuri Gagarin. When he returned to earth, one of the statements he made was that he "looked for God, but did not see him." For him, it was another evidence for the atheistic Communism philosophy. A Christian somewhere replied, "If he had stepped out of that space suit, he would have seen God in a hurry!"

Let me move on to a second question. People have often asked me, "When we get to heaven, will we know each other?" I'm surprised that so many people think of the inhabitants of heaven as one large, grey mass of "sameness." They think we lose our features, our genders, and our personalities. What do you say about that?

We will definitely know each other in heaven! There are several passages in the scriptures that teach this. For instance, when King David's infant son died, David said, "I shall go to him, but he cannot return to me."[4] Jesus promised His disciples at the Last Supper that He would eat with them again.[5]

When Jesus, Peter, James, and John were on the Mount of Transfiguration, Moses and Elijah spoke with the Lord.[6] The three disciples easily recognized the Old Testament men. This is more evidence we will know one another in heaven.

Because we will know each other there, does that mean we will live together in families? That seems to be a natural conclusion. If I am going to recognize the people I loved most on earth, I think I'm going to want to be near them throughout eternity. I'm told that one of the blessings of heaven is never having to say "goodbye" to loved ones or friends. In heaven, there is no more separation.

You're right, Dad. The hope of being reunited with deceased loved ones is one of the tools God uses to keep His people focused on heavenly things while living on earth. Those living are to never forget that they are citizens of two worlds—the earth and the kingdom of God. Certainly God expects His children to be fully engaged in this world. We all have important jobs to do in service to the Lord and one another. However, it is too easy to fall in love with this life and forget that it is preparatory for the one to come. Longing to see deceased loved ones is good because it brings a balance to living in two worlds.

Let me mention another passage. On one occasion, Jesus spoke of heaven as his "Father's house in which there are many rooms,"[7] indicating, I think, that there will be plenty of space for dwelling together. If there are many inhabitants in close proximity in heaven, it seems natural to me that this would be referring to family and close friends. The fact is, Dad, that much of the learning we spoke of earlier will take place in context with our family and others we know.

That leads to a very important question that comes from persons who have lost their long-time spouse. They say, "Jesus taught that in heaven there is no giving or receiving in marriage.[8] Does that mean I'll be without my deceased husband (or wife)?" What about that Van? Do husbands and wives become like sisters and brothers in heaven, or do they maintain their status as husband and wife?

You can know for certain, Dad, that God has made heaven the place of perfect joy and contentment. He knows what will best satisfy His people in heaven. If it is being in close proximity with spouse, children, or parents, He will see to it.

But the Bible says there is no marrying in heaven.

That's not to say that those already married will be separated. True, there will be no need for procreation in heaven. But remember, our good relationships on earth, those that enrich and bless us, will not be taken away in heaven. Rather, they will be *made more perfect*. First and foremost, of course, will be our relationship with God. However, as is true on earth, relationships in heaven with others will also be of great importance. If the marriage relationship is dismissed in heaven, do you think all other relationships will be minimized or erased there?

Look at it this way, Dad. When you play golf with your friends, each of you fills a certain role. You dress a specific way, having to wear golf shoes and other clothing appropriate to the game and required by the golf club. You follow golf rules and use language specifically connected to this game you love so much. *But,* once you walk off the course and drive away from the club, you dress, talk, and relate differently. Nonetheless, you still have an on-going relationship with your "foursome."

That's the way it is between husband and wife in heaven. There may be major differences in the couple's interactions here and their interactions there, but they will still be together and the relationship in heaven will be much richer.

Okay. But what if a person has been married, widowed, and remarried? Who will be that person's spouse in heaven?

God will have things worked out in heaven so that there will be an answer to that question. You can rest assured that no one will be sad or feel left out in the home God has prepared for His people.

That's not as clear as I would hope for. However, let me ask a more difficult question. Will there be sex between husband and wife in heaven? After all, that is one of the most important aspects of a relationship between husband and wife. If I read *The Song Of Solomon* correctly, sex between husband and wife is for more than procreation. It is one of God's greatest gifts to His people.

In heaven, God withholds nothing from His people that will contribute to their greatest joy. If He chooses to eliminate the sexual relationship between a husband and wife, it will be because He has something much better for His people whom He loves so much!

Van, that's not a "yes or no" answer!
You'll find out soon enough. Meanwhile, do all you can to reassure people who ask you about husband-wife relationships in heaven. Remind them that God has prepared the best possible existence for them in their eternal home.

Family! I want so badly to be with my family in heaven!
Dad, ten million years from today your mom will still be your mom. She'll be able to talk to you in ways that only a mother can talk to her child. Ten billion years from now, you'll be able to gather around a table at a Thanksgiving meal with your family, the same way you do today. The real difference will be that when you have that Thanksgiving dinner in heaven, everyone you remember from your childhood will be there.[9] Talk about family relationships in heaven!! You can't fully imagine, Dad, what it's going to be like!

What about pets, son? Will those who have a dearly loved dog, cat, horse, or other animal be with them in glory?
Did you know that there are over one hundred and twenty species of animals named in the Bible?[10] Think about Noah and the ark. And what about the manger scene when Jesus was born? Then, there's Jonah and the big fish. These are just a few examples of how important animals are in the activities of God.

My point is, yes, there will be pets in heaven. Once again, the principle is *whatever it takes for us to fully experience the joys of eternal life, our gracious God will provide for us.*

These are helpful answers, Van. What about those saints already in heaven? Do they see us here on earth and know what we do?
The answer to that one, Dad, is "yes" and "no." It is true that citizens of heaven can step from eternity back into time for specific

purposes. In Hebrews 12:1, believers on earth are likened to athletes running a race. The "cloud of witnesses" who observes this struggle is the Saints in heaven who have finished the race and are encouraging their brothers and sisters on earth to persevere.

An additional reason you can know those in heaven have the option of seeing what is occurring here on earth is the concept of "time travel" that we previously discussed. You'll be able to enter anywhere on the "time-line" of earthly life you choose to explore.

Won't that make people there sad when they see their loved one suffering? What if they observe a child or parent behaving in an unseemly manner? It seems to me that could take away some of the joy of heaven.

Dad, keep in mind that what happens here on earth is seen from God's perspective, not earth's. He sees things in context. He understands the heart of those engaged in behavior of whatever type, bad or good. Moreover, He sees the end results. In the same way, the saints of heaven also see things more broadly. That is not to say that sinful behavior is excused; it is not. God has His ways of enabling us to deal with these issues.

Now, back to your question about citizens of heaven being able to see what is going on here on earth. As we discussed earlier, eternity has already begun from heaven's perspective. With that understanding, we see that there is no "life on earth" to view. Unless the heavenly citizen has reason to travel back in time, like I am doing in this conversation with you, the saints in heaven are not regularly looking down on earth.

Let's shift gears, Son. We are told in scripture that the Saints of heaven will serve the Lord.[11] What kind of work will we do there?

The worship of God will, of course, occupy much of our time there. Worship will be not be *required* of us so much as we'll have a strong *desire* to praise and adore Him.

You're right, though. Much of our time in eternity will be in service to God. We will gladly accept the role of servant there. And remember, the greatest compliment God could pay to Moses was to refer to him as "my servant."[12] Moses' successor, Joshua, was not referred to as "God's servant" until much later, after he had proven himself even more.[13] The point is, to be a servant of God is the highest honor conferred upon a person.[14]

What, exactly, will we do in heaven to serve the Lord? Christ told a parable in which he said the faithful would be given authority over cities.[15] The reference is both to the thousand-year reign of Christ on earth during the Millennium and could be a glance into what our service will be like in heaven.[16] After all, Dad, our eternal abode consists not only of the city of God (heaven proper), but millions of galaxies never discovered by humans. The servants of the Lord in heaven will have authority over those far-flung expansions of eternity.

In what ways, exactly, do we serve in the galaxies?

God will give each of us some kind of oversight of our designated place of service. When Adam and Eve were in the perfect state of innocence in the Garden of Eden, God told them to oversee the garden.[17] The original plan of our Heavenly Father was for His people to rule over all aspects of creation. Sin entered and spoiled all of that, of course. But in the new "Garden of Eden," we will once again be placed in authority and our fulfillment will come in gladly serving in that capacity.

In addition, Dad, our service to the Lord in heaven will be in keeping with our gifts, abilities, passions, and interests. After all, those are the qualities God put into us when He created us, so He will place us in a "hand-glove" setting to serve Him. Expertise will be magnified and there will be heightened creativity in each of us.

Work in heaven sounds like fun to me!

Absolutely! Whenever we can do something that is in keeping with our capabilities, it is pleasurable and the work is more diversion than toil. As a result, we'll never grow tired or find ourselves without ambition for the job to be done. On earth, the older a person becomes, the less skilled he or she becomes. The opposite is true in heaven; with time, the worker becomes more and more effective in service to God.

Another topic of great interest to many is that of angels. What will be our relationship to angels in heaven?

One thing that may surprise many people in heaven is that there are billions of them! Every one of them, as is their task now, will be to serve God in heaven.

They'll be our companions in service?

Not on the same level. God has made angels to be servants of man as well.[18] They serve the Lord by ministering to our needs, most of the time in ways we do not recognize.

Some people see angels as kind of "mini-gods."

That is unfortunate, and the product of writers, artists, and magical thinking across the years. Some people even worship angels or pray to them. There are times in the Bible, and more times than we can number throughout history, when angels have responded when someone has prayed to God for help.[19] But to make angels the destination of our prayers is a mistake. We have direct access to God Himself because of Jesus' death removing the barrier between the Lord and us.[20]

I remember a man saying once, half facetiously and half-truthfully, "You need to ask your guardian angel which stock to buy."

It is important to be aware of such dangers. The temptation is for people to see angels as kind of "magic wands" they can wave and use to meet their selfish desires. This opens the door to dangers because Paul teaches that demons may present themselves as angels.[21] This is the trap of the New Age movement where adherents are ensnared and latch on to a "spirit-guide." These false angels then lead them further and further from Christ and the truth.

Where did angels come from, Van? Were they, as God, always in existence?

No, they are created beings, and like human beings, the Creator gave them free will. They have the ability to choose between what is right and what is wrong. The Bible refers to them as "the heavenly host."[22] At one point, millions of these angels rebelled against God and there was a war in heaven.[23] Satan and his force of angels were expelled from heaven and these fallen angels became what the Bible calls demons. The obedient angels, on the other hand, have continued as God's servants to this present time.

So are angels in heaven, or here on earth with us?
Both. Legions of them serve God and worship Him in heaven while many of them are here on earth to serve God's people.

You have said we need to be careful not to worship nor pray to angels. How are we to relate to them? How, specifically, do they minister to us?
Fortunately, the Bible gives plenty of material showing the work of these creatures. We see angels guarding the Tree of Life in the Garden of Eden after God banished Adam and Eve.[24] An angel intervened when Abraham was about to sacrifice his son, Isaac.[25] It was an angel who warned Joseph that he should take Mary and the newborn Jesus to Egypt in order to escape Herod who wanted to have the baby killed.[26]

There was a time once when I felt very strongly that I was protected by an angel.
Tell me about it, Dad.

I know it is very subjective on my part, but when we lived in San Antonio I had an experience that really frightened me. I was on my way home from the church one afternoon. I was eastbound on a road where I had the right-of-way and the north-south traffic crossing the road had stop signs. I was on the top of an incline and could not see crossing traffic. As I topped the hill, a car came flying past the stop sign on my right. I hit my brakes immediately as the other car swerved around me, never slowing down. *In that moment, I had a very strong sense that an angel had protected me. I said out loud, "The Lord sent an angel to keep me from getting hit."* **I know this could be conjecture on my part, but to this day I am convinced it was an angel!**

It is certainly possible, Dad. One day, if God wants us to have that information, we might be surprised to learn of hundreds of times, if not thousands, angels did something like that to help us.

Let me move to a related question. Angels, like all believers, will worship and serve God in heaven. Does that mean we are all on the same level there? To put it another way, will everyone in heaven experience the same amount of contentment and happiness?

This requires another "yes and no" answer. It is true that everyone in heaven will experience indescribable joy. Heaven will not be heaven if perfection is not found on every hand. No one going to heaven need fear having "second class" status there.

However, not everyone there will receive the same degree of rewards. Never forget: the Christian's desires and works on earth will have heavenly consequences. Each of us will be judged and compensated according to his or her obedience to God's will.[27]

So Billy Graham will be more richly rewarded than the average church member? After all, Mr. Graham has preached the Gospel to more people than any other person who has ever lived.

No, no! Not at all! Judgment in heaven of our works for the Lord will be based on how the Lord gifted us and what He expected of us. God gave Billy Graham the gifts to be a world-evangelist. He expected Mr. Graham to preach all over the world, on television, and so forth. Mr. Graham will receive whatever rewards the Lord gives him because of his level of obedience to God's plan for him, not because he has had so much more visibility in the world. On the other hand, the man or woman whom God intended to live in a less visible world and was given fewer talents with sparse opportunities will not be judged in the same way that Billy, you, or I will be judged. Look at it like this, Dad. If you and five-year old grandson Dylan were helping Mom clean the garage, and there were items to move from one place to the other, you would handle the heavier ones and he would be expected to do much less. If he did nothing, you or Mom would tell him he had to help. He is being "judged" for what he is capable of doing in comparison to you. You too are being judged accordingly. If you don't do more work or lift heavier items than Dylan, something would be wrong.

I understand what you are saying.
We know clearly that we are not made righteous with God by doing good works. Our hope of eternal life is dependent on the death and resurrection of Christ and our embracing Him as Savior.[28] That, however, does not lessen our responsibility to do as much good as we can. In fact, busily doing good deeds is what pleases the Lord.[29]

Here is an acrostic that will help explain what I'm saying. Rewards in heaven are based on how the child of God handles his or her "MOAT."[30]

"M" represents our money. How did we use the resources God placed in our hands? Did we follow the philosophy and practice of many in thinking our material goods were to be lavished upon ourselves, or did we see our possessions as gifts from God for the welfare of ourselves *as well as a means of blessing others*?

The god of materialism is very powerful and lives in the hearts of many. The Christ-follower is not exempt! Jesus warns us, "Be on your guard against all kinds of greed"[31] and boldly states, "You cannot serve both God and money!"[32]

Have you ever seen the bumper sticker: "He who dies with the most toys wins?" It is more correct to say, "He who dies with the most toys still dies—and never takes his toys with him."[33]

How we handle our possessions in this life will have an important role when we stand in judgment! That's good insight.
More than we usually understand, Dad.

"O" stands for opportunities. In life, the Christian is given many opportunities to serve others. We can do this in our church, in our neighborhood, at work, at school, or wherever the door is opened to us. God will reward us in heaven according to how we served Him by serving others here on earth. Jesus made it very clear that when we meet the needs of others, as opportunity allows, *we are in fact serving Him!* If we choose to look the other way and not really care about the hurting, the lost, the hungry, the confused, He says we are *failing Him*.[34]

"A" refers to the abilities God has given us. Christians are given talents or capabilities that enable us to more effectively serve Him and others. The Bible refers to these gifts in several passages.[35] As you know, Dad, the point is to learn what our abilities are, develop and utilize them in serving others within the context of our church family.

"T" is for time. The issue is how do we utilize days, weeks, months, and years in a way that honors God? Is our time usage such that it blends with His plan for us in this world? God will judge and reward us accordingly.

Okay, I can more clearly understand how God rewards His people in heaven. Obviously, not all Christians will be on the same level of faithfulness in how they use the "MOAT" God has given them. So, will there be second-class citizens of heaven?

Not at all! Even the person who makes it "by the skin of his teeth" will be overwhelmed with contentment in heaven!

Look at it like this: you can take two glasses, one small, one large. Fill both of them to the brim with water. Which of the glasses is full? Obviously, both of them. But one will hold more water because it has a greater capacity.[36] In the same way, some inhabitants of heaven will have a greater capacity for God's rewards, a capacity developed by strong faith, obedience, and extraordinary service to the Kingdom of God. The lady with just two spiritual gifts may more effectively serve the Lord on the earth than the woman with five talents, but chooses to utilize only three of them.

In the parable of the widow's offering, Jesus teaches that a poor person may give more than a wealthy person even though, as in this story, the widow's amount is less in terms of total "dollars."[37] Why is this true? Because she gave all she had; the wealthy person gave, percentage-wise, much less. Who, in heaven, will receive the greater reward for giving between these two people?

One last question, Van. What about contentment in heaven when a family member or close friend chooses to reject God's

love and is eternally separated? After all, God does not force people to love Him and to embrace His son as their Lord.

People have struggled with that concern for centuries! There have been several suggestions put forth; let me share a few of them and then tell you how I think this issue will be resolved.

There are those who teach that our memories will be "blocked" in heaven in the sense that we will never remember that person. It will be as though they were never born as far as our awareness of them is concerned. An analogy would be having a brother or sister you never knew (they were adopted by someone else and your parents never told you). Though they are real people, they do not exist as far as you are concerned.

Some have suggested that God will, in the end, allow even the vilest people who have ever lived to come into heaven. This position is called "universalism" and teaches there is neither hell nor possible separation from God.

You mean that God just "overlooks" the evil deeds of people like Adolph Hitler or Saddam Hussein or Osama bin Laden?

Not necessarily. Some of the proponents of universalism would say these kinds of evil people will suffer in the future life (not in heaven nor hell) for their sins, but that their suffering will be remedial in nature, and that through suffering they will be purified from sin and finally delivered from it.[38]

What is your position on this question?

Jesus taught that some people would choose the "broad way to destruction" over the "narrow way to life eternal."[39] My view is that we will see these people through the eyes of God; that in heaven we will learn to hold the same attitude toward them that God will have. I think we will be thrilled for every person present, and for those not there, we will have an understanding that is like God's perspective and it will make sense.

I said I had one last question earlier, but there is another one that comes to mind as we talk. What about the multitudes of people who have never had an opportunity to hear of Jesus

Christ? And what about babies who die as infants? Lastly, any word about those who have lived for many years, yet their minds never developed beyond that of a small child?

The last part of the question is easy, Dad. Infants, whether in years or in mental development, are innocent and will be with the Lord in heaven.

The first part of the question, however, is much more difficult. Let me encourage you to leave that to God who is just, loving, and more than fair in His mercy and grace. What the scriptures make clear is that when an opportunity comes to hear and respond to the good news of Jesus, His reasons for coming to earth and how He will bring us to God, the choice is ours to accept or reject. If we accept, we will be given entrance to heaven as members of the family of God. If we willfully reject God's offer of salvation and eternal life, we have chosen the consequences of that refusal. These two aspects of being "found" or being "lost" are clearly taught in the scriptures. The great mass of mankind lying in between these two classes we can safely leave in the hands of God. It is God's prerogative to decide what is to be done with the person who has never heard the gospel, nor given an opportunity to hear.[40] In the meantime, Christians are mandated with the responsibility of doing all we can to get the message of salvation to every single person in the entire world.

One last word, Dad: we will have an eternity to thoroughly research these and millions of other questions in the heavenly information center!

CHAPTER 13—SOON, AND VERY SOON....

I have an obsession! I cannot get away from it, nor do I want to! Anytime I hear of the death of a person, my mind immediately fixes on the question, "Did that person go to heaven or hell when he/she died?" This morning, Lilly Faye and I were watching the news while sipping our coffee. The announcer reported that the day before, a well-known sports personality had died. Some of the comments made included, "It's for the best. His crippling disease would have taken more and more of his vitality." Someone else said, "He lived a full life during his fifty years on this earth. He was able to do the things he set out to do as a young man and no one should lament his passing." But I thought, "Where is his soul right now? If with God, then we can all rejoice that he has reached his eternal home and is out of pain. If eternally separated from God, the torment he experienced on earth is nothing compared to the pain of being forever lost!"

Death notices or obituaries in the paper always raise those questions in me. How can we possibly believe in heaven or hell and the eternal aspect of that existence, yet place much more emphasis on *this* life rather than the one to come? As someone has said, we think of ourselves as bodies that have souls while we should more correctly think of ourselves as souls that have bodies.[1] Paul laments, "If our gospel is veiled, it is veiled to those who are perishing. The god of this age has blinded the minds of unbelievers, so that they cannot see the light of the gospel of the glory of Christ."[2] Spiritual blindness will disable persons and make it impossible for them to take the long look at this life and eternity.

Nonetheless, death is inevitable. As C.S. Lewis observed, the statistics on death are impressive—so far it is one out of one.[3]

Max Lucado is more graphic when he reminds us of death's reality: "Death!! The bully on the block of life. He catches you in the alley. He taunts you on the playground. He badgers you on the way home: 'you too will die someday.'

"You see him as he escorts the procession of hearse-led cars. He's in the waiting room as you walk out of the double doors of the intensive-care unit. He's near as you stare at the pictures of the bloated bellies of the starving in Zimbabwe. And he'll be watching your expression as you slow your car past the crunched metal and the blanketed bodies on the highway. 'Your time is coming,' he jabs.

"Oh, we try to prove him wrong. We jog. We diet. We pump iron to escape it, knowing all along that we will only, at best, postpone it.

"'Everyone has a number,' he reminds us, 'and every number will be called.' He's so persistent. He'll steal the joy of your youth and the peace of your final years. He'll make you so afraid of dying, you'll never learn to live!

"That's why we need a Big Brother to fight the bully! That Big Brother is Jesus, and when He resurrected, He sealed the death of death. 'Oh death, where is your sting? Oh grave, where is your victory?'"[4]

I know it is possible to be morbid or become over-focused on death. This is unhealthy. God wants us to embrace life and live it to the greatest level possible. Jesus said He had come into the world with the purpose of helping us find abundant life.[5] Yet we can be certain that we are not ready to experience life to the highest level if we have not given thought to our mortality. It is foolish to live as though one is going to exist in this earthly life forever! Entertainer Ray Charles is quoted as saying, "Live every day like it's your last, 'cause one day you're gonna be right."[6] (Note: Ray Charles died six months later!)

Speaking of *when* one is going to die, there is information available that can help us to have at least a general idea of when our time on earth is up. If you live in Zambia, the average length of life is 36. In Japan, it's 76. In the USA, it's 73.[7] Persons who study these kinds of statistics have recently been given more help. Longevity researchers at Harvard Medical School and Boston Medical Center have developed what they call the *Living to 100 Healthspan Calculator*. A questionnaire based on one's lifestyle and family history feeds data into a computer. After some crunching of numbers and profile information analysis, you are presented with your personalized life span, down to the decimal point. There is even information given as to possible changes one can make to enhance their chances of living longer on this earth.[8]

American culture seems to have mixed feelings about death. Books on the subject have proliferated recently. Here are a few titles:

Tuesdays with Morrie by Mitch Albom (Doubleday)

The Handbook for Mortals: Guidance for People Facing Serious Illness by Lynn and Harold (Oxford University Press)

The Grace Of Dying by Kathleen Dowling (Harper San Francisco)

Will The Circle Be Unbroken? by Studs Terkle (Ballantine Books)

Talking About Death Won't Kill You by Virginia Morris (Workman Publishing Company)

So, on one hand, interest in knowing more about death and what may follow is growing. Yet apathy rules with the larger percentage of people who cope with the thought of death and the afterlife by not thinking about it at all. Newsweek magazine points out this paradox relative to the subject: "Though Baby Boomers have passed fifty, still much of American culture is exhibiting a touch of denial."[9]

Since the issue of death is of utmost interest and importance, there are two questions we want to ask: "What happens to us immediately at death?" and "How can we be confident we are ready to embrace death when it comes calling?"

Christian teaching about death and afterlife includes the Old Testament perspective with an expanded treatise on the subject in the New Testament. The basic thrust on death in the Old Testament is that there is a correlation between dying and sin. According to Genesis 2:17 and 3:19, death is a direct result of sin. Generally speaking, death and the future life are somewhat gloomy themes in the Old Testament. The religion of the Hebrews was primarily related to this life, not life after death. In fact, there are only a few passages in the Old Testament that clearly propose death with life thereafter.[10] On the other hand, the continuance of life on earth was the mark of God's favor.[11] Elderly people were to be respected, in part, because there is a good chance they had lived a godly life and were reaping the benefits of such.[12] To see your children's children was the prayer of the righteous person in the Old Testament.[13]

When we get to the New Testament, we know from certain passages that Jesus, Peter, and Paul all believed that the Old Testament taught the continuance of life after death.[14] In addition, the overall outlook on death and the life hereafter is transformed. Now, the evil of death has been overcome and death is looked upon as not as a hole into which one falls, but a passageway to a more abundant and glorious life! It is of interest that Jesus, Luke, and Paul refer to death as "sleep," with the intent of stressing rest, peace, and awakening.[15] In the story of The Rich Man and Lazarus, Jesus shows He does not regard death as the end of consciousness, but the entrance into something wonderful for the child of God.[16] Paul is eager to remind the Believer that death is one of the things that cannot separate us from the love of God.[17]

Clearly, the Christian who embraces the teachings of the Bible as God's definitive word on the subject of death and the afterlife finds great comfort in what God has planned for His people. Theologian W.T. Conner gives three New Testament reasons the Believer can have great confidence in the face of death and what follows:

1. The resurrection of Jesus over death;

2. The communion (i.e., possibility of daily fellowship and personal relationship) with God that comes to people through faith in the crucified and risen Redeemer;

3. The teachings of Jesus on the subjects of life, death, and the hereafter.[18]

Erwin Lutzer contrasts Shakespeare's *Hamlet* ("To be or not to be") and the Apostle Paul's assertion that he is ready to live or die.[19]

He shows how Hamlet contemplates suicide and finds it both attractive and repulsive. If he knew for certain that death would rid him of all his troubles, he would embrace it. However, he fears what might await him in the afterlife. Lutzer summarizes his comparison in these words:

"Hamlet says, 'Live or die, I lose!' Paul says, 'Live or die, I win!!' What a difference Christ makes!"[20]

Back to the question asked at the beginning of this chapter: what happens at the time of dying?

Consider first the question from the perspective of those who are left behind. There will probably be a memorial service. The funeral serves as an opportunity to bring family and friends together to honor the deceased. Memories of happier days past can be momentarily relived during this time as eulogies recall the deceased's life. From the Christian viewpoint, the goal will be to encourage hope in the midst of sadness. Those present are reminded that the deceased may be physically gone from us, but he or she is more alive than ever because of the honored position as a Christ-follower. The family and friends can be encouraged to lift their spirits by looking to the day when they can be reunited for eternity with their loved one who has died.

Actually, the funeral does not really affect the deceased in any meaningful way except on *this side* of death. It may mean much for us while we are alive to think about what we may want said or done at our funeral. I read today the comment of Jackie Burke, the eighty-one year old golf professional who has been described as "Golf's greatest living sage"[21]: "Live your life so that when you die, you fill up the church. A big funeral says something about how much you were loved, or at least respected. These people who get to the church by way of the electric chair don't get much of a turnout. They have to rent the pallbearers."[22] However, the one who has gone from this dimension to the eternal one will have much more important things to deal with than how many people may be at his funeral! The fate is now sealed! What one has done to prepare for eternity is the only possible issue of importance. Anthony DeStefano writes, "We must always try to remember that God is primarily concerned with one thing: whether or not we make it to heaven. Next to that awesome question, everything else means nothing. If you die at ten years old in an automobile accident, and go to heaven, then you had a successful life. If you die peacefully in your sleep at ninety, rich and powerful in the eyes of the world, but go to hell, then your life was a wasted tragedy."[23]

After the memorial service, there is a time of adjusting to the loss of the loved one. For some people, that is a short time and daily activities quickly return to routine activities. For others, the adjustment can take a much longer time. The conventional wisdom is that a widower or widow will need eighteen to twenty-four months to fully adjust to the loss of a spouse. Obviously, some people will need much, much longer and some, unfortunately, are never able to get over the death of a husband or wife. The same can be said about a child. The many factors that affect one's adjustment to loss by death are varied and not the purpose of this material. For those who do have a more difficult time, it is wise to lean heavily on family, friends and a Christian counselor. (Lilly Faye and I have been helped in the loss of Van by family, friends, church, and Christian counseling to head off depression issues. In addition, we have been active in a wonderful organization called "Compassionate Friends."[24]

Then, from the perspective of the deceased Christ-follower, what happens at death?

For one thing, the act of dying is not necessarily a bad experience. True, some people die in great pain because of the circumstances of their death. But I remember Professor John Newport saying in seminary class that studies have revealed that, by and large, the actual experience of taking one's last breath is not a traumatic experience. When the act of dying is seen from this viewpoint, it is easy to understand why portions of the Bible refer to death as "sleeping."[25]

In the closing hours of Van's life on earth, I watched his face! He was unconscious, breathing in a shallow but unlabored manner. His body was not tense; there was no grimace on his face. When the time came, he just stopped breathing. Though we were in deep grief at that moment, he seemed to be at peace.

Methodist pastor Charles Allen has written a little book entitled <u>When You Lose a Loved One</u>. In one of the chapters, he references an article by nine physicians who discuss "How Does It Feel to Die?" One of the men, Dr. William Osler says, "Most human beings not only die like heroes, but, in my clinical experience, die really without fear or pain." Another of the nine had this comment, " I use the word *sweetness* in connection with death. As a doctor who has seen many people expire, I know it is often sweet to die. Frequently I have seen a change of expression as the moment of death approached, almost a smile, before the last breath was taken. What one may see at the point of death will probably remain an eternal mystery. But it should remain, too, a vision with no terrors for any of us."[26]

In one of the churches I served as pastor, there was a good man, one of the deacons, who told of almost dying in an accident at the foundry where he worked as a welder. In the moments just before losing consciousness, he said he came face to face with the reality that he would probably die in the next few minutes. I have thought many times of his description of those crucial moments before he fell into unconsciousness: " I felt a strange peace. I said, 'Lord, I'm coming to you. Please watch over Dorothy and the boys.' I was unafraid and fully ready to accept my fate. The next thing I knew, I awakened in a hospital room."

Professor Newport told us that day in seminary class, "God in His grace and love for humankind seems to have ordained that when it comes time for us to leave this earth, it is not as traumatic for the dying person as we fear."

Randy Alcorn's <u>Dominion</u> gives the account of what could happen to the Believer at the moment of death:

"Dani Rawls awoke again, this time not to a scene of agonized confusion but to a glowing quiet passageway. Behind her lay a land of shadows, a gray and colorless two-dimensional flatland. Ahead of her lay something that defied description.... a fresh and utterly captivating place, resonating with color and beauty.

She could not only see and hear it, but feel and smell and taste it, even from a distance. The light beckoned her to come and dive into it with abandon, as cool water beckons on a blistering August afternoon.

A Voice From Heaven

Already everything within her told her this was the Place that defined all places, the Place by which all places must be judged. It reached out to Dani, playfully grabbing at her, drawing her soul as a powerful magnet draws iron filings.

'The colors. So many colors!' In comparison to this, all the colors of earth she'd enjoyed so much had been no more than shades of gray. Now there was an infinite rainbow of colors, reaching as far beyond earth's rainbow as sunlight beyond a match flame.

'I'm getting stronger. I can feel it.'

Only minutes ago she'd been so weary, bone tired, the way she'd felt many nights caring for her sick children, alone, without a husband...How was she moving so quickly while still feeling too drained to move?

Wait. She was being carried. Carried in giant arms. How could she not have realized it until now?

She turned her head and looked up at a sculptured face. Who was this?

She stared at his arms, brawny and strong. The muscles were taut but not bulging, suggesting he wasn't taxed by her weight, that she was a light burden or that he was used to bearing heavy ones. Maybe like her slave forefathers. She was thankful for his strength and felt her own body infusing with energy.

She remembered her Bible. Lazarus was carried to heaven by angels. Was this an angel sent to carry her home? A slightly unnatural grin broke across his marbly face. 'Hello Dani.'

'Who are you?' she asked. 'An angel sent to get me?'

'Not sent to get you. Beckoned to take you. I've been with you all along. We're both going home.'

'Home? You mean...home, like in the Bible?'

'Just like in the Bible.'

'I didn't hear a trumpet sound.'

'The trumpet comes later, at the return and the resurrection. This is not that day. This is the day of your exodus from mortality to life.'"[27]

Many people have given testimony of having had a "near-death" experience. During this time, the person actually dies, yet is later resuscitated and gives glowing reports of a wonderful experience.

A Voice From Heaven

Some of the common traits reported by these people include seeing a bright, warm light, sometimes identified as an angel or as Jesus Christ; having their senses on "super-alert" in that the colors and sounds around them are much more beautiful and dramatic than in real life; and often having to make a tough decision of going on into eternal life or returning to earthly life. These people almost always come back with a heightened love for people and for the things of God. Some in medical or psychological (as well as religious) fields criticize these events as dynamic gymnastics of the mind in a time of crisis. Others have embraced the experience as valid and worthy of study for insights into what may happen at the time of death.

Betty Malz has written an account with similar characteristics of what she saw and experienced when she was pronounced dead by medical personnel. It was 5:00 A.M. when she "died." Hospital attendants removed all life-support tubes from her body and covered her with a sheet. Soon after, unaware that his daughter had died, Betty's father came into the hospital room. For "several minutes" he stood at her bedside, weeping and praying. Then he noticed a slight movement of the sheet, and behold, his daughter sat up, eyes wide open. Without the need of tubes being reinserted and feeling very hungry for the first time in weeks (her body weight had dropped to 85 pounds), family and medical personnel pronounced her "alive."[28] Some refer to Betty Malz's experience as that like Jarius' daughter.[30]

Paul spoke of what would happen to him at death. Even during times of difficulty and persecution, his affirmation was firm. "We never give up. Our bodies are gradually dying, but we ourselves are being made stronger each day. These little troubles are getting us ready for an eternal glory that will make all our troubles seem like nothing. Things that are seen don't last forever, but things that are not seen are eternal. That's why we keep our minds on the things that cannot be seen.

"Our bodies are like tents that we live in here on earth. But when these tents are destroyed, we know that God will give each of us a place to live. These homes will not be buildings that someone has made, but they are in heaven and will last forever. While we are here on the earth, we sigh because we want to live in that heavenly home. We want to put it on like clothes and not be naked.

"These tents we now live in are like a heavy burden, and we groan. But we don't do this just because we want to leave these bodies that will die. It is because we want to change them for bodies that will never die. God is the one who makes all of this possible. He has given us his Spirit to make us certain that he will do it. So always be cheerful!

"As long as we are in these bodies, we are away from the Lord. But we live by faith, not by what we see. We should be cheerful, because we would rather leave these bodies and be at home with the Lord."[30]

Back to the issue of what happens to the Believer at the moment of death. Jesus' encounter with the repentant thief on the cross gives us a starting place to find the answer. The dying man had asked, "'Jesus, remember me when you come into your kingdom.' Jesus answered him, 'I tell you the truth, today you will be with me in paradise.'"[31] The Apostle Paul made mention of this teaching that at death the Christian goes directly into the presence of God. "We are confident, yes, well pleased rather to be absent from the body and to be present with the Lord."[32] This passage indicates that believers will be with Jesus after their death.

Throughout the centuries, Christians have experienced death as a part of the human race. Some have died peacefully, in their bed at home with family and friends in attendance. Some have died more violently in accidents, persecutions, war, terrorist's attacks, or muggings and killings. Obviously, others have died in a multitude of ways considered neither peaceful nor violent. But all conscientious followers of Christ have died with this hope in their hearts: "Who shall separate us from the love of Christ? Shall tribulation, or distress, or persecution, or famine, or nakedness, or danger, or sword? As it is written, 'For your sake we are being killed all the day long; we are regarded as sheep to be slaughtered.' No, in all these things we are more than conquerors through him who loved us. For I am sure that neither **death** nor life (emphasis mine), nor angels nor rulers, nor things present nor things to come, nor powers, nor height nor depth, nor anything else in all creation, will be able to separate us from the love of God in Christ Jesus our Lord."[33] Nothing, certainly not death, can separate the Believer from the heavenly Father. As He is with us on earth, we will be with Him in heaven.

Of course, there are explanations other than the Judeo-Christian view of what happens when one dies. Some people, perhaps a growing number of them (or a growing vocal expression of this group), believe that when we die, that is it. No life; no nothing! We evolved from this earth and our bodies will decompose back to the origins of life. Tom Stoppard writes, "Death is not anything... it's the absence of presence, nothing more.... the endless time of never coming back...a gap you can't see."[34] This secularist's view encourages the dying person to find comfort in the fact that all die, remember the good times, and make peace with yourself and with your fellow man so that you go into oblivion with no regrets. Life is like a long-weekend that comes to an end far too soon, and the goal is to enjoy it while you can.

Another view is that of the Reincarnation position. Hinduism and certain forms of New Age philosophy subscribe to the idea that all forms of life are eternal, no matter if it is a human, animal, or vegetation. Nothing dies in the sense that it ceases to exist; it just changes matter and returns to earth in some other form. Shirley MacLaine, actress, singer, dancer, and author of nine books that have sold more than twenty million copies, describes what she calls the **Big Truth**: "Nothing and no one ever dies; it just changes form."[35] In her eclectic manner, very common to New Age thinking, Ms. MacLaine borrows from several religions and eastern philosophies to make her case that life, death, and reincarnation is the true pattern of life and death.

However, the purpose of my book is to promote the Christian teaching that the Christ-follower is taken to his eternal home in heaven! The climax of existence is *eternal destiny!!*

A wonderful book by Nancy Pearcey entitled <u>Total Truth: Liberating Christianity from its Cultural Captivity</u> identifies three indicators of how humankind seeks to make sense of life. One's worldview is revealed by the answer given to three questions:

1. Creation: what does this person think is the origin of the world?

2. Fall: What does this person think is the source of human problem?

3. Redemption: What does this person think is the solution that would put things right?[36]

The answers to these questions will reveal

(1) Does this person believe God is creator or is our world the result of some non-deist evolutionary processes? If God is involved in the creation, He must surely be involved in what happens at death.

(2) There are major problems that have confronted humankind since the beginning of time. In spite of all our technological, scientific, and other cultural-educational advances in life, we still face hatred among people, lying, killing, wars, the strong taking advantage of the weak, etc. Does one's worldview allow the presence of sin in the life of each of us? If so, how is the sin problem going to be addressed?

(3) The third question causes us to ask if the reply of conventional wisdom is the answer. That would include but not be limited to:

.... better education among the masses

.... a fairer distribution of money between the "haves" and the "have-nots"

.... or, more effective medicine to correct behavioral problems.

Let it be noted that the way the Christian worldview answers those three questions is radically different from the answers given by the agnostic, atheist, World Religions, or New Age worldviews.

The point of preceding material is to say that I would include a fourth question To Ms. Pearcy's penetrating inquiries:

(4) Eternity: What does this person think happens after death? Is there "life after life," or should we not think about any life other than the one we have right now on earth? If there is an eternity in another dimension, how does that relate to us?

This leads to yet another big question each of us must ask: *Since heaven will be indescribably wonderful, how can I be certain I will go there when life comes to an end for me on earth?*

Unfortunately, some people say we cannot know for certain; only hope. Across the many years I have been in ministry, I have asked many people if they were ready for death, ready to meet God. The majority of replies have been "I sure hope so." The humility behind such an answer could reveal one's sense of awe in the presence of such an overwhelming idea as death and the life thereafter. That spirit is commendable. The fear of coming across as a pompous "know-it-all" also tends to encourage understatement. We have seen too many shallow and gaudy "religious people" flaunting their super-spirituality for selfish gain and we don't want to be identified with that group. It is true, unfortunately, that some Christians speak too quickly, having given little thought to what they are saying and the way they are being perceived. (George W. Bush, on the occasion of his 40th month in the presidency, met with a small group of Christian journalists and discussed a variety of issues. When asked about how he expresses his Christian faith, he said, "I have a fantastic opportunity to let the light shine. I will do so, however, as a secular politician. My job is not to promote a religion but to promote the ability of people to worship as they see fit." He also said, "You can't use your faith as a shallow attempt to garner votes. Otherwise, you'll receive the ultimate condemnation."[37]

Then, there are those persons who actually *resent it* when someone declares he or she is confident of going to heaven when death comes. That has always intrigued me. They say, "I don't know for sure about life after death and I don't want you to tell me that you are certain you are going to heaven!" These are the folks who tell us that one's religion is personal and private. Could this attitude reflect one's preference for insecurity about what happens when we die? There are people who find comfort in knowing that everyone (else) just "hopes" to make it to heaven. In his book The Gospel According To The New York Times, reporter William Proctor has a chapter entitled, "The Seven Deadly Sins...According to the Times." He writes, "Perhaps the greatest threat to the social and political agenda of the New York Times is conservative religion, especially evangelical Christianity... If you claim certainty or assurance in your faith, you're on thin ice with the *Times*. The paper is much more comfortable with church and synagogue members who say they are still searching for truth, or who express some skepticism or doubt about traditional religious doctrines.

"In contrast, those who say they are certain about their beliefs are likely to be dismissed by the paper as 'fundamentalists,' or 'biblical literalists'—or even 'zealots,' or 'bigots.'"[38]

The Bible teaches, however, that faith makes it possible for one to have an inner assurance about our eternal destiny. "My purpose in writing is simply this: that you who believe in God's Son will know beyond the shadow of a doubt that you have eternal life, the reality and not the illusion."[39] In John's gospel account, he addresses the ultimate purpose of Jesus' miracles while on earth. He writes, "Jesus did many other miraculous signs in the presence of his disciples, which are not recorded in this book. But these are written that you may believe that Jesus is the Christ, the Son of God, and that by believing you may have life in his name."[40]

Sadly, Paul's words to the Ephesian church are apropos to some in this day: "Remember that you were at that time separated from Christ.... strangers to the covenant of promise, having no hope and without God..."[41] There are at least two barriers to a person connecting to Jesus Christ and finding eternal life.

One is the concept of universalism, the idea that all people are God's children already (whether they know it or not). There is no hell; everyone who is ever born will eventually be in heaven. Shirley MacLaine takes this idea one step further. "Guilt is a kind of living hell. Guilt is based on a feeling of having sinned, but what is sin? There is no such thing as sin. We are all part of God.... people's perception that they have sinned is an illusion they have created."[42]

When one embraces this position, all thoughts (usually) are focused on this world, not the one to come. Worship, prayer, reading, and seeking to understand the scriptures are all "electives" in the school of life. While it may be better to live a good life, sin is also of no consequence except of what it may do to us while on earth. There is no judgment and no reason to think about how our choices in this life will affect our eternity.

(This doctrine can also impact the true Christ-follower, for "when the heart no longer feels the truth of hell, the Gospel passes from *good news* to just news. The intensity of joy is blunted and the heart-spring of love is dried up."[43])

Closely related to universalism is "annihilationism"—the belief that hell does not involve eternal conscious misery but is the cessation of existence. "Okay," some say. "Really bad people do not deserve to spend eternity in heaven with God. However, their "hell" is, when they die, they simply go into non-existence." As with universalism, this philosophy of eternity also takes away any motivation to seek after God in this life as preparation for the one to come.

Another barrier that can keep a person from a true relationship with Jesus Christ is the teaching of "Works Salvation." Here, you become a Christian by being a good, moral person. As part of your goodness, you go to church, do kind and helpful deeds for others, and live an exemplary life. You vote, pay your bills on time, and try to live by the Golden Rule. You stand out among others as a truly good person.

The person who lives this kind of life is to be congratulated and admired. Much of the welfare of our society depends on this type of person. Most communities around our nation have a large number of these people and are good places to raise a family.

Christians will do well to have these qualities. The Bible makes it clear that God expects His children to reflect these as well as other virtues. In fact, the Bible goes so far as to teach that a person who says he is a Christian yet lacks these basics attributes is fooling himself! The New Testament book of James insists that if we have real faith, we will show it by acting in the right ways. Topics in this portion of the Bible include anger and quarrelling, showing favoritism, controlling the tongue, boasting, caring for widows and orphans, patience, and prayer.[44]

The great theologian of the Bible, Paul the Apostle, usually divided his writings into (a) the theological - theoretical basis of his teachings and (b) the practical results of believing these teachings. Christian teachings include both *Believe* and *Behave*. (See the book of Romans as an example with Chapters 1-11 theological teachings and chapters 12-16 the practical results)

However, it is extremely important to remember that the Christ-follower does good deeds because he has a relationship with Christ and wants to be obedient, and not in order to achieve salvation. This is a significant theological truth that even many Christians and church-attending people never seem to grasp: our right-standing before God is not because of our good deeds, but because of what He has done for us. The biblical doctrines of Atonement (Christ's death on the cross for our sin), Justification (being declared forgiven by God) and Righteousness (the state of spiritual innocence) are what God does for us, not what we do for Him in our good deeds.

I heard a pastor once tell of how he described in summary statements the differences between Christianity and other religions: "Do" and "Done."[45] *Do* refers to the things I mentioned earlier—the need to perform good deeds and, in the process, win the acceptance of God and a place in heaven. By doing good things, we are able to "convince" God to love and accept us. The spotlight, thus, is on the *goodness* of the person.

However, *done*, according to Pastor Bill Hybels, emphasizes what God has (already) done for us. He has given His Son as the sacrifice for our sin, (Romans 5:6-11) then sends His Holy Spirit to "awaken us" to our need (John 16:8,) and to His willingness to forgive us, and empower us to become Christ-followers. It is His grace that gives us both the *desire* and the *power* to hear and respond to Him.[46]

The simple, yet theologically profound way God has chosen to bring a Believer into His family has been described as easy to embrace as the ABC's of life:

A—acknowledge your need of God's cleansing. "All have sinned and fall short of God's glory." (Romans 3:23)

B—believe in your heart that Jesus' death on the cross was to pay for your sin. Believe that His resurrection vindicates His power over life and death and that He will give you eternal life when you embrace Him. (John 3:16-18; I Peter 1:17-23)

C—confess Him to yourself and to others around you. Let it be known that you are a Christ-follower. (Romans 10: 8-11)

A "sinner's prayer" could be something like this: "Dear God; thank You for helping me to see Your love and Your plan to give me eternal life. I confess that I am a sinner and ask Your forgiveness. I turn away from my sin; please forgive me for the things I have done to hurt You, others, or myself. I embrace Jesus Christ as my Savior and, through Your power, will make Him the Lord of my life from now on. Thank You for hearing my prayer. Amen"

The Christian's privilege and responsibility is to strongly encourage others to learn of God's plan of salvation and embrace it. The consequences are eternal in nature! Time is short for all human beings on this earth and we cannot be certain of when our time to die will come. That is the reason the writer of Hebrews says, "now is the time, behold today is the day of salvation. If you hear His voice, do not harden your heart."[47]

"*The Makropulos Case* is an opera about a woman who, as a result of a chemical elixir, was enabled to live on and on. On January 5, 1996, the Metropolitan Opera was to present its first performance of Leo Janacek's work at Lincoln Center in New York City.

As the lights dimmed and the curtain opened, a lawyer's clerk was singing as he climbed a ladder leaning against a huge filing cabinet. The words to his light-hearted song were, 'Too bad you can only live so long.' Suddenly, he released his hold on the ladder and fell backward to the floor. Many in the audience thought this attention-grabbing scene was part of the presentation, when in fact the singer, Mr. Richard Versalle, had suffered a heart attack and was probably dead before he ever hit the floor! Naturally, the presentation was cancelled and everyone filed out of the opera house in a somber mood. What a startling picture it was to all who could see it: mankind's desire to live longer on the earth, musing over the possibilities, and dying at that very moment! Unfolding once again was the ageless story of the brevity and uncertainty of life against the backdrop of the universal longing."[48]

God has placed that longing in our spirits. He prepares us for life after death. It is another expression of His grace, seeking to awaken us to the imperative need of turning to Him right now!!

"No eye has seen, no ear has heard, no mind has conceived what God has prepared for those who love Him."

The Apostle Paul (I Corinthians 2:9)

REFERENCES

Section I Introduction

1. J. R. R. Tolkien, *The Lord of the Rings: The Fellowship of the Ring* (New York: Ballantine Books, 1955), 102.

Chapter 2—Restoring the Years

1. C. S. Lewis, *The Chronicles of Narnia: The Voyage of the "Dawn Treader"* (New York: Collier Books, 1952), 136.
2. James 5:16.
3. 2 Samuel 11:1-27.
4. Psalm 32:3-5, 7 Contemporary English Version.
5. William Gaither, *"Because He Lives"* 1971.
6. Genesis 50:20.

Chapter 3—The Road Back Home
1. John 3:3.
2. T. W. Hunt, letter to author, June 2003
3. Dr. Jeffrey Satinover, *Homosexuality and the Politics of Truth* (Grand Rapids MI: Baker Books, 1996), Front Cover.
4. Ibid. 113-117.
5. Ibid. 184-185, 189-190.
6. Ibid. 187.

7. Dr. David Finkelhor, "The Problem of Pedophilia," *The National Association for Research and Therapy on Homosexuals*; available from http://www.narth.com/docs/pedophNEW.html 1998; Internet. Accessed 3 August 2006.
8. Dr. Jeffrey Satinover, *Homosexuality and the Politics of Truth*, 44.
9. Alan Chambers, interview by author, July 2003.
10. Dr. Jeffrey Satinover, *Homosexuality and the Politics of Truth*, 222.
11. James 4:7.
12. Exodus International, http://www.exodus-international.org/.
13. Ephesians 6:10-20.

Chapter 4—Joy and Grief Together
1. Charles Dickens, *A Tale of Two Cities* (New York: Barnes & Noble Books, 1859), 7.
2. 1 Thessalonians 4:13.
3. Marvin Olasky, "Whistling Past the Graveyard," *WORLD Magazine*, 7 July 2002.
4. Ibid.
5. Erwin W. Lutzer, *One Minute After You Die* (Chicago: Moody Press, 1997), 58.
6. Marvin Olasky, "Whistling Past the Graveyard."
7. Philippians 4:19 King James Version.
8. Francis A. Schaeffer, *How Should We Then Live?* (Wheaton, IL: Crossway Books, 1976).
9. Hebrews 9:27.
10. Revelation 14:13.
11. Genesis 49:33.
12. T. S. Eliot, *East Coker, No. 2 of "Four Quartets,"* 1940.

Chapter 5—Life Is Not a Dress Rehearsal
1. Blair Masters, Scott Williamson, "*Jesus Doesn't Care*," (Word, Inc.: 1996).
2. Philip Yancey, *What's So Amazing About Grace?* (Grand Rapids, MI: Zondervan Publishing House, 1997), 70.
3. 2 Corinthians 12:7-8.

Chapter 6—Lessons Van Taught Me
1. 2 Corinthians 4:16 King James Version.
2. Robert Robinson and John Wyeth, *"Come Thou Fount,"* 1759.

Chapter 7—Vanisms
1. Philip Yancey, *What's So Amazing About Grace?*, 70.
2. Joe Dallas, *Sermon on Homosexuality*, City of Katy, First Baptist Church, Katy, c. 1999.
3. Wayne Martindale, Jerry Root, *The Quotable Lewis* (Wheaton, IL: Tyndale House Publishers, 1990), 272.
4. Matthew 19:16-22.
5. Psalm 103:11-12, Jeremiah 31:34.
6. Revelation 12:7-10.
7. Arthur Travis, Classroom lecture, The Institute of Religion, Texas Medical Center, Houston, TX, 1973.
8. Jonah 3:1-3.
9. James 4:13-15.

Chapter 9—Sermons From the Heart
1. *Compact Oxford English Dictionary*, 3rd ed., s.v. "prodigal."
2. D. Stuart Briscoe, *The Communicator's Commentary: Genesis* (Waco, TX: Word Books, Publisher, 1987), 307.
3. Daniel 9:16.
4. Genesis 25:21-28.
5. Josh McDowell, *The Last Christian Generation* (Holiday, FL: Green Key Books, 2006), 81.
6. James 15-16.
7. D. Stuart Briscoe, *The Communicator's Commentary: Genesis*, 324.
8. Genesis 39:21.
9. Ibid. 42:6.
10. Ibid. 37:20-22.
11. Ibid. 43:34.
12. Ibid. 44:4b.
13. Ibid. 42:24b.
14. Ibid. 42:25.
15. Ibid. 44:33-34.

16. Ibid. 45:7-8.
17. Ibid. 49:33.
18. Ibid. 50:20-21.
19. Malachi 4:5-6.
20. Raymond Brown, *The Bible Speaks Today Series: The Message of Nehemiah* (Downers Grove, IL: InterVarsity Press, 1998), Back Cover.
21. Jeremiah 29:4-9.
22. Ezra 3:1-4:5.
23. Harry Kemp Quote, available from http://en.thinkexist.com/quotes/harry_kemp/; Internet. Accessed 3 August 2006.
24. Nehemiah 2:4-9.
25. Ibid. 2:11-16.
26. Ibid. 3:1-32.
27. Ibid. 3:1.
28. Ibid. 3:1-32.
29. George Patton Quote, available from http://www.generalpatton.com/quotes.html; Internet. Accessed 3 August 2006.
30. Nehemiah 3:5.
31. Ibid. 4:1-23.
32. Ibid. 5:1-13.
33. 1 Peter 5:8.
34. Ephesians 6:10-18.
35. Nehemiah 6:15.
36. Ibid. 9:1-36.
37. Matthew 5:4.
38. Galatians 6:9.

Foreword to Section III
1. Peter Kreeft, *Everything You Ever Wanted To Know About Heaven* (San Francisco: Ignatius Press, 1990), 9.
2. Randy Alcorn, *In Light of Eternity* (Colorado Springs: Waterbrook Press, 1999), 4.
3. Augustine Quote, available from http://en.thinkexist.com/quotes/saint_augustine/2.html; Internet. Accessed 3 August 2006.
4. Dana Blanton, "Fox Poll: More Believe in Heaven Than Hell," 28 October 2005: available from http://www.foxnews.com/

story/0,2933,173838,00.html; Internet. Accessed 3 August 2006.
5. John F. MacArthur, *The Glory of Heaven* (Wheaton, IL: Crossway Books, 1996), 9.
6. John Piper, *Brothers, We Are Not Professionals* (Nashville: Broadman and Holman Publishers, 2002), 116.
7. J. Oswald Sanders, *Heaven: Better By Far* (Grand Rapids, MI: Discovery House Publishers, 1993), 18-20.

Chapter 10—A Voice From Heaven
1. Luke 16:19-31.
2. Psalm 91:11-12.
3. *Beyond the Gates of Splendor*, Jim Hanon, 20th Century Fox DVD, 2005.
4. *This Is Your Life*, Auca speaking on TV show, c. 1978.
5. Revelation 7:17.
6. Luke 7:36-50.
7. Robert H. Stein, *The New American Commentary: Luke* (Nashville: Broadman Press, 1992), 236.
8. C. S. Lewis, *A Grief Observed* (San Francisco: Harper San Francisco, 1994), 68.
9. Erwin W. Lutzer, *One Minute After You Die*, 92.
10. 1 Corinthians 13:12.
11. 1 John 3:2.
12. John 20:24-28.
13. Acts 1:9.
14. Ibid. 7:55-56.
15. W. T. Conner, *The Gospel of Redemption* (Nashville: Broadman Press, 1973), 347-348.
16. Ibid.
17. Mark 10:15; Luke 18:17.

Chapter 11—Time and Eternity
1. John Piper, *Brothers, We Are Not Professionals*, 114.
2. Revelation 21:25.
3. 2 Peter 3:8.
4. Exodus 3:14.

5. John 8:52-59.
6. Matthew 19:26; Mark 10:27.
7. Peter Kreeft, *Everything You Ever Wanted To Know About Heaven*, 169.
8. Ibid. 198.
9. Ibid. 168.
10. Exodus 3:14.
11. Hebrews 11:40b, The Message.
12. Revelation 6:10-11 The Message.
13. Ray Stedman, Recording of sermon "Life Beyond Death," (Palo Alto, CA: Discovery Publishing), Dec. 1, 1969.
14. Iris Blue, Personal testimony, City of Katy, First Baptist Church, Katy, c. 2001.
15. 1 Samuel 17:1-51.
16. Exodus 14:5-29.
17. Matthew 28:2-10.
18. Elizabeth Sherrill, *All The Way To Heaven* (Grand Rapids, MI: Fleming H. Revell, 2002), 173.
19. C. S. Lewis, *Out of the Silent Planet* (New York: Collier Books, 1965).
20. Peter Kreeft, *Everything You Ever Wanted To Know About Heaven*, 185-186.
21 Revelation 21:1-27.
22 Matt Redman, *"The Heart of Worship,"* (Kingsway's Thankyou Music, 1999).
23 Randy Alcorn, *Deadline* (Sisters, OR: Multnomah Books, 1994), 50.

Foreword to Chapter 12
1. 1 Corinthians 2:9.

Chapter 12—Questions And Answers
1. John 14:2-3.
2. Ibid. 3:1-13.
3. Ed Young, *In My Father's House* (Houston: Winning Walk Family, 2001), 4-6.
4. 2 Samuel 12:23.

5. Luke 22:17-18.
6. Matthew 17:3-4.
7. John 14:2-3.
8. Matthew 22:29-30.
9. Anthony DeStefano, *A Travel Guide To Heaven* (New York: Doubleday, 2003), 61-62.
10. Ibid. 80.
11. Revelation 22:3-4.
12. Joshua 1:1-2
13. Joshua 24:29.
14. Mark 10:35-45.
15. Luke 19:17-19; 1 Corinthians 6:2-3.
16. Revelation 20:1-4.
17. Genesis 1:26-18, 2:15.
18. Hebrews 13:2.
19. Daniel 22:10-12.
20. Matthew 27:51; Hebrews 4:14-16, 10:9-22.
21. 2 Corinthians 12:14-15.
22. Jeremiah 33:22; Luke 2:13.
23. 2 Peter 2:4; Jude 6; Revelation 12:7-9.
24. Genesis 3:24.
25. Genesis 22:11-12.
26. Matthew 2:13.
27. 2 Corinthians 5:10.
28. Ephesians 2:2-9.
29. Ibid. 2:19.
30. Ed Young, *In My Father's House*, 13-15.
31. Luke 12:15.
32. Matthew 6:24.
33. Randy Alcorn, *The Treasure Principle* (Sisters, OR: Multnomah Books, 2001), 38.
34. Matthew 25:31-46.
35. Romans 12:3-9; 1 Corinthians 12:1-31; Ephesians 4:11-16.
36. Anthony DeStefano, *A Travel Guide To Heaven*, 137-138.
37. Luke 21:1-4.
38. W. T. Conner, *The Gospel of Redemption*, 353.
39. Matthew 7:13-14.

40. W. T. Conner, *The Gospel of Redemption*, 354.

Chapter 13—Soon And Very Soon
1. Dr. Stuart E. Lease, "The Veracity of Scripture," Scripture-Centered Ministries available from http://www.libertycamp.org/SCM/Messages/5.HTML; Internet. Accessed 3 August 2006.
2. 2 Corinthians 4:4-5.
3. C. S. Lewis, *The Weight of Glory* (San Francisco: Harper San Francisco, 2001), 61.
4. Max Lucado, *Six Hours One Friday* (Nashville: W. Publishing Group, 2004), 100-101.
5. John 10:10.
6. Ray Charles Quote, The Reader's Digest, January 2004
7. Author Unknown, "Life Span," Available from http://www.efmoody.com/longterm/lifespan.html; Internet. Accessed 3 August 2006.
8. John Murgensen, "Do The Math," *The Houston Chronicle*, 16 August 2004, Star section. Also see www.livingto100.com.
9. Marvin Olasky, "Whistling Past the Graveyard."
10. Job 19:26-26; Isaiah 26:19; Daniel 12:1-3; Ezekiel 37:1-14.
11. Isaiah 38:18-20.
12. Psalm 21:1-7.
13. Psalm 126:6.
14. Mark 12:24-27; Acts 2:25-28; Acts 13:33.
15. John 11:11; Acts 7:60; 1 Corinthians 15:20.
16. Luke 16:19-31.
17. Romans 8:38.
18. W. T. Conner, *The Gospel of Redemption*, 305-306.
19. Philippians 1:21-24.
20. Erwin W. Lutzer, *One Minute After You Die*, 142.
21. Guy Yocom, Interview with Jackie Burke, *Golf Digest Magazine*, May 2004, 119.
22. Ibid.
23. Anthony DeStefano, *A Travel Guide To Heaven*, 165.
24. See: www.compassionatefriends.org
25. 1 Thessalonians 4:13-14.

26. Charles L. Allen, *When You Lose A Loved One* (Westwood, NJ: Fleming H. Revell Company, 1959), 18-19.
27. Randy Alcorn, *Dominion* (Sisters, OR: Multnomah Books, 1996), 87-89.
28. Betty Malz, *My Glimpse of Eternity* (Waco, TX: Chosen Books, 1977), 81-83.
29. Mark 5:22-24, 35-43.
30. 2 Corinthians 5:6-8 Contemporary English Version.
31. Luke 23:42-43.
32. 2 Corinthians 5:8 New King James Version.
33. Romans 8:35-39 New American Standard Version.
34. Marvin Olasky, "Whistling Past the Graveyard."
35. Shirley MacLaine, *Out On A Leash* (New York: Atria Books, 2003), 46.
36. Nancy Pearcey, *Total Truth: Liberating Christianity From Its Cultural Captivity* (Wheaton, IL: Crossway Books, 2004), 83-87.
37. Marvin Olasky, "Still Standing," *WORLD Magazine*, 5 June 2004.
38. William Proctor, *The Gospel According to the New York Times* (Nashville: B & H Publishing Group, 2000), 114-115.
39. 1 John 5:12-13 The Message.
40. John 20:30-31.
41. Ephesians 2:12.
42. Shirley MacLaine, *Out On A Leash*, 134.
43. John Piper, *Brothers, We Are Not Professionals*, 113.
44. James 1:19-21, 26-27; 2:1-9; 3:1-12, 13-16; 4:13-17; 5:7-11, 13-18.
45. Bill Hybels, Sermon on "*Do and Done*," Fort Worth, TX, 1990.
46. Philippians 2:13.
47. Hebrews 3:7-8.
48. Elizabeth Sherrill, *All The Way To Heaven*, 198-199.